D1241443

WORLD WAR ONE IN THE AIR

A PICTORIAL HISTORY

World War One in the Air

—— A Pictorial History ——

Ken Delve

Acknowledgements

First published in 1997 by
The Crowood Press Ltd
Ramsbury, Marlborough
Wiltshire SN8 2HR

© Ken Delve 1997

All rights reserved. No part of this
publication may be reproduced or
transmitted in any form or by any means,
electronic or mechanical, including
photocopy, recording, or any information
storage and retrieval system, without
permission in writing from the publishers.

**British Library Cataloguing in
Publication Data**

A catalogue record for this book is
available from the British Library.

ISBN 1 86126 080 6

Typeset by M Rules
Printed and bound in Great Britain
by Butler & Tanner Ltd, Frome, Somerset

My deepest thanks go to my friend and
respected aviation authority Peter Green;
without his help this book would not have
come to fruition. Others whose help I grate-
fully acknowledge include Andy Thomas,
Brian Pickering (of MAP), the ever helpful
and efficient staff of the Air Historical
Branch, the *FlyPast* magazine archive,
Richard Chapman and Heinz Birkholz (*Jet
& Prop*), Jack Bruce, Ken Wixey, Dennis
Hylands, Harry Holmes, Stuart Leslie, Alex
Imrie and the Imperial War Museum.
Ken Delve, December 1996

Contents

The Birth of Air Power

Following the war in North Africa between Italy and Turkey, during which the former used aeroplanes for the first time, it was stated that 'a new weapon is born: the aircraft! A new battlefield is created; the air! A new chapter is opened in the history of warfare; the chapter of aerial warfare!'

When Europe went to war in August 1914 it proved to be a conflict that changed the face of the military art – new weapons were brought into use that meant that nineteenth-century strategies and methods of warfare were no longer viable. The most significant changes on land involved greater destructive potential as provided by such devices as the machine gun, but more significant for the future was the appearance of the aeroplane. Air power had arrived. True, it was slow to develop but by 1916 the aeroplane had come of age and was being employed in a variety of roles far exceeding the original concept of 'airborne eyes'. By the time of the Armistice in November 1918 all the major fighting powers had large air forces and the aeroplanes bore little resemblance in their capabilities to those that were available just four years before.

It has not been possible to include much reference to the all-important role of the training establishments of the various participants, although the photographs shown do provide a more extensive consideration of this aspect of the air war. Likewise, most operational consideration is given to the Western Front – particularly British and German developments – and there is only brief mention of the colonial warfare operations that took place on the periphery of the war.

Above: **The Avro 504 saw operational service in several roles early in World War One, and later became one of the most important training types used by the RFC and later the RAF. This particular example served with the Robert Smith Barry School of Special Flying at Gosport.** (Harry Holmes)

Below **Pfalz E.II 454/15. The Pfalz and Fokker 'Eindecker' monoplane fighters were the world's first truly successful fighters and had a profound effect on the development of air power.** (Heinz Birkholz)

CHAPTER ONE

1914–15

War was declared on 1 August 1914 between Germany and Russia. France declared war on 3 August and Britain the following day. Many commented that it would be 'over by Christmas' and so it was – but by Christmas 1918, not 1914. Britain, as always, was confident in the capability of her sea power to protect her global interests while at the same time being able to influence the course of any European land war. France was confident, indeed over-confident, in the capability of her apparently impressive army. Prussian-dominated Germany was confident of repeating the stunning victory over France in 1870. It was seen by all the major protagonists as a land war in which the 'mass and manoeuvre' of land armies would prove decisive. Little real thought was given to the third dimension – air power.

At the outbreak of war the notional air capability of the participants was not very impressive, with most of the major European powers having something in the order of 300 aircraft, by no means all of them being 'operational' types. The Royal Flying Corps (RFC) had four 'operational' squadrons capable of being deployed to France, Nos. 1 to 4 Squadrons; the first aircraft moved to Dover on 12 August ready to fly to France in support of the British Expeditionary Force (BEF). The following day, the honour of being the first British aircraft to land in France went to BE2a '347 of 2 Squadron flown by Lt. H.D. Harvey-Kelly – who subsequently rose to the rank of Major, was awarded the DSO but died of wounds received after an air combat on 29 April 1917 while serving with 19 Squadron.

By 15 August all the units were at Amiens and placed under the command of Brig.-Gen. Sir David Henderson; at this stage he had 63 aircraft of mixed types. The following day the squadrons moved to Mauberge, and the first reconnaissance mission was flown on 19 August by Capt. P.B. Joubert de la Ferté in a Blériot of 3 Squadron and Lt. G.W. Mapplebeck in a BE2 of 4 Squadron.

Aeroplanes were at this time seen as little more than extensions of the light cavalry that had for generations been the eyes of the army, and this reconnaissance role was the rationale for their presence in the various military services – most of whom had, often reluctantly, seen the value of these machines during pre-war exercises. The reconnaissance role was to remain central to air operations throughout the war and many of the other roles that subsequently developed came about as a result of needing to protect one's own reconnaissance while at the same time denying reconnaissance to the enemy.

The RFC was soon to score its first major success in the provision of timely reconnaissance to the land force commanders. With the German forces making a rapid advance, the Allied armies were forced to retreat from the positions at Mons, the BEF II Corps taking up positions along the Conde-Mons canal with I Corps moving up to take the right flank and the French 5th Army to the right of them. On 22 August the RFC units flew twelve vital reconnaissance sorties that revealed a German enveloping movement and the collapse of the French position on the Sambre – it was imperative that the BEF should retire in sympathy or risk being destroyed. The reconnaissance aircraft continued to monitor the growing threat and observed that by 23 August both flanks of the BEF were in danger; the Battle of Mons began on this day, the retreat was ordered and the BEF was saved.

German aircraft were also active and before long the two sides came into contact with one another. However, the first 'victory' went to the RFC on 25 August when three BE2s of 2 Squadron chased a Taube. The German pilot elected to land in a field, at which point Lt. Harvey-Kelly landed nearby and he and his observer, Lt. W.

Mansfield, chased the enemy pilot into a wood. They were unable to catch him but returned to the Taube and set fire to it before climbing back into their BE2 and returning to base. The greatest danger to aviators of both sides at this time was, apart from the unreliability of their aircraft, that of ground fire from infantry of both sides and on the same day a BE2a of 4 Squadron was damaged by French infantry fire.

The Germans launched an attack over the Somme in late August, trying to find the weak spots in the Allied defences. The all-important reconnaissance task continued and when Gen. von Kluk tried to wheel his 1st Army to the south east this was spotted and reported, enabling the Allied armies to conform to the manoeuvre. Nevertheless, the German advance continued. By 2 September they had crossed the Oise and it appeared that they might be preparing to rush to Paris – as in 1870. French aeroplanes from the Paris citadel unit were also watching the German armies and making reports of their movements.

Reports of the first few days of September stating that the Germans had wheeled east of Paris were not at first believed until other aircraft brought confirmation – Gen. Joffre and his HQ staff were among the many sceptical Army commanders. However, when he at last gave credence to the reports and realized that Paris was not in danger and that the enemy was sweeping towards the Marne, he acted upon them and launched his counterstroke; he was then quick to appreciate the value of the small number of RFC aircraft: 'please express most particularly to Marshal French my thanks for the services rendered to us every day by the English Flying Corps.'

The French had entered the conflict with some 132 aircraft in their 'front-line units', these being attached to the major Armies (1st to 5th) and the Cavalry Corps. The majority of units were equipped with Henri-Farman (4 squadrons), Maurice-Farman (5 squadrons) or Blériot (4 squadrons) types, although some had Voisins, Caudrons, Breguets or Deperdussins. In common with French practice throughout the war the squadron nomenclature included the initial letters of the type with which it was equipped, so Henri-Farman units at this time were HF1, HF7, HF13 and HF19, whereas Blériot units were BL3, BL9, BL10 and BL18.

Following the important role that aircraft had played during this critical Battle of the Marne, Joffre instituted a number of changes, including appointing Cdt. Joseph Barès as aviation chief to the French High Command. It was also decided to form additional units from aircraft that had been ordered by overseas nations but that were still at the manufacturers.

The German Air Service had entered the conflict with 33 'field units' (Feldflieger Abteilungen or FA), each with six aircraft, attached to the eight Army HQs and 25 Corps HQs on the Western and Eastern fronts. In addition, ten 'fortress flights' (each of four aircraft) were formed at such places as Metz and Cologne. Thus, the German air resources were spread thinly.

Airships

The German High Command also had six airships as a 'strategic reconnaissance' (and bombing) force; three each being allocated to the two fronts (Z4, Z5 and SL2 to the Eastern Front; Z6, Z7 and Z8 to the Western Front, with Z9 being added in August). The first mission was flown on 6 August 1914 when Z6 bombed targets at Luttich; however, it was an inauspicious start as the Zeppelin was damaged by ground fire and eventually had to crash-land in a forest near Bonn where it was eventually dismantled. Other raids in August were equally disappointing, with little damage being caused to French military targets while Z7 and Z8 were hit by ground fire. However, Z9 had a somewhat more successful outing on 21 August when it flew along the coast bombing Antwerp, Zeebrugge, Dunkirk, Calais and Lille.

With their origins in the last decade of the nineteenth century, airships – especially those designed by Count Ferdinand von Zeppelin – played a significant part in air operations during the First World War. Although all the major belligerents employed airships for military purposes, it was those of Germany that were most active

and the best remembered. The German Army acquired its first Zeppelin in August 1909 and was soon investigating the limits of its military potential. By the outbreak of the war the German Army and Navy were operating airships, primarily in the reconnaissance role but with the additional task of bombing; it was to be these vessels that opened a new dimension in warfare with the start of aerial strategic bombing.

The main aircraft types in use by the Allies in this first part of the war were little more than adaptations of the most basic aerodynamic principles (but it was only just over ten years since the first powered flight by the Wright Brothers!). The monoplane Blériot XI was in widespread use by the French, with a small number also in service with the British, and for the Germans there was a similarly simple, but far more attractive, aircraft in the Taube, with its bird-like wings. Both were quite suitable for gently flying around observing the ground – in relatively peaceful conditions. The same was true of the fragile-looking Henri-Farman and Maurice-Farman types that the French and English also used.

Although the German aeroplanes had no doctrine of strategic bombing, a Taube of IX Corps, flown by Hermann Dessler, 'attacked' Paris on August 29; the pilot flew around the Eiffel Tower and dropped a number of small bombs near the Gare de L'Est, killing one civilian. Similar raids were mounted up to mid October by which time 16 sorties had been flown and 56 bombs – none bigger than 10lb (5kg) – had been dropped. Individualism was to be a feature of air operations by all participants for the first year of the war, including personal modifications to aircraft and self-generated missions.

However, as with the RFC's operations, it was in the field of reconnaissance that aircraft were proving to be of the greatest value; for example, German aircraft monitored the French retreat from the Maas in late August enabling the ground troops to switch the direction of their attack. Although very few aircraft had been allocated to the Eastern Front, they proved of immense value due to the great distances involved and the lack of German cavalry. The German counter-stroke against the initial Russian offensive proved masterly and, during the last week of August, led to the battle of Tannenberg and the virtual destruction of Gen. Samsonov's Second Army. This battle had involved some 300,000 men and so the small scale of the

air involvement, in terms of numbers, must be put into perspective.

The Royal Naval Air Service (RNAS) had instigated coastal air patrols from bases such as Great Yarmouth to cover the area from the Humber to the Thames searching for enemy shipping, especially minelayers. Although other locations, such as Ostend, had been used to help cover the area, the Admiralty also converted three channel steamers – the *Empress*, *Engadine* and *Riviera* – to carry seaplanes for operations in the North Sea. September saw the acquisition of the old Cunard liner *Campania*, which was converted to act as a seaplane carrier for the Grand Fleet, although it was not commissioned into service until the following May.

It was not only the German fleet that was seen as a threat by the Royal Navy; the employment of airships for long-range reconnaissance gave the Germans an advantage that the Royal Navy found disconcerting. The RNAS, however, had a broad appreciation of the potential offensive nature of air power and, in true Nelson fashion, had decided that the best means of defence was attack. Thus the Eastchurch Squadron moved to Ostend on 27 August (becoming 3 Squadron RNAS with effect from 1 September) with the intention that 'the primary duty of naval aeroplanes now became the location and attack of any airship sheds which the Germans might erect within 100 miles radius of Dunkirk.' Under the aggressive leadership of Cdr. Charles Samson the RNAS units, including their 'armoured car sections', were soon to make their presence felt.

On 6 September Gen. Joffre launched his counter-stroke causing an immediate German retreat. The increasing value of air reconnaissance, and its appreciation by Corps commanders, had led to greater calls for its employment at all levels. The RFC responded with an organizational change whereby pilots reported direct to the appropriate Corps HQ (I or II Corps). By 9 September the Germans were back across the Marne, having been warned by their reconnaissance aircraft of the danger; a few days later the Allied reconnaissance aircraft reported in turn that strong trench lines had appeared at Chemin des Dames. The Battle of the Aisne, launched on 14 September, was one of the first that involved very heavy artillery barrages and the employment of trench defences. It was a fiercely fought contest in which neither side gained an upper hand – trench warfare had arrived and was to dominate the Western Front for the next four years.

On 15 September, Lt. G.F. Pretyman of 3 Squadron carried out the first photographic reconnaissance mission. He exposed five plates, two of which showed the promise of the technique. To the land commanders it was the power of artillery that was seen to be the battle-winning weapon and it was therefore vital to make the artillery as accurate as possible. The use of aircraft and balloons for artillery spotting was to become one of the primary roles for the new air services as an extension to their existing reconnaissance role.

One of the major problems was that of how to co-ordinate the artillery. A variety of techniques were tried, such as the use of coloured lights and, from late September, trials on the use of wireless telegraphy. The latter led, on 27 September, to the formation of HQ Wireless Section (which later became 9 Squadron). The Germans had also been experimenting with wireless telegraphy in co-operation with Telefunken & Huth. The first operational systems were in use on the Western Front by December 1914, although for both air arms this was still very much in its infancy and not widely available.

Meanwhile, the RNAS had launched the first British raid against German territory when, on 22 September, two aircraft went to attack the airship sheds at Düsseldorf and two to attack those at Cologne. Only Lt. C.H. Collett of 1 Squadron RNAS found his target and he dropped three bombs on the Düsseldorf target from 400ft (120m); it seems that two may have hit the target but neither exploded. All four aircraft returned safely to Antwerp. Eager to achieve a success in this offensive bombing campaign, a second attempt was made on 8 October when Sq. Cdr. Spenser Grey tried unsuccessfully to attack the Cologne shed but had to bomb the railway station instead.

Lt. Reggie Marix in Sopwith Tabloid '168 had a much more successful mission. He arrived over the Düsseldorf sheds and attacked, dropping his bombs from 600ft (180m) and scoring a direct hit – the shed collapsed in flames, destroying the new Zeppelin Z9. He recalled the attack:

I had a good trip and got to my destination without incident. But the shed was not where I had expected to find it, and my map had been wrongly marked. So I had to fly around a bit, which excited some interest. I was at 3,000ft and some AA opened up, but well wide of the mark. I found the shed further away from the town than expected. I closed, and as soon as I was sure of my target I put my nose down and dived with my engine still on. One would not normally do this as it puts an awful strain on the rotary Gnome as the revs go up . . . when I was at about 500ft I released the two bombs, one after the other, and began to pull out of the dive. I had kept my eyes fixed on the shed but I vividly remember the rapid points of flame as the ground machine guns opened up. As I pulled out of my dive I looked over my shoulder, and was rewarded with the sight of enormous sheets of flame pouring out of the shed. It was a magnificent sight.

The ground defences had damaged the aircraft and Marix was forced to land short of his base – he eventually made it back by train and bicycle! This was without doubt the first success for what would later be called 'strategic bombing' and as such was very important in the development of air power, although not recognized as such by many at the time.

The RNAS were not the only ones to see the potential of the aircraft for bombing the enemy at home. On 19 October Maj. Wilhelm Siegert was appointed as aviation adviser to the German High Command; he formulated and had approved a plan to create a bomber force to attack England. The Ostend Carrier Pigeon Unit (Brieftauben Abteilung Ostende) was originally intended to comprise two 18-aircraft wings to be based at Calais to attack military targets in southern England. The failure to capture Calais led to a modification of the plan, with Ostend becoming the main base.

The unit was primarily equipped with Albatros and Aviatik types and for the remainder of the year was used to bomb targets in France such as Dunkirk, Nieuport, Furnes and La Panne:

These Ostend squadrons were composed of the best and most experienced pilots from every other branch of the air force. To increase their mobility they were quartered in rail carriages and carried out their first raids from an aerodrome in Flanders. From this base they undertook their first attacks on Dunkirk and other objectives behind the 4th Army Front. In the spring of 1915 they were removed to the Eastern Front, and at the same time an additional squadron was formed that was known as the Metz carrier Pigeon Squadron after the name of their first aerodrome. [P. Neumann, *The German Air Force in the Great War*]

Daylight attacks became too hazardous as air defences were strengthened and so the unit switched to night attack with a consequent loss of accuracy.

The first German to have bombed England was apparently Lt. Karl Kaspar who, on 25 October, claimed to have attacked Dover in his Taube of Abteilung 9. The French too had been keen to try out their aircraft in the bombing role; as early as 14 August Lt. Cesari with Cpl. Prudholm-Meaux had attacked the airship sheds at Metz. However, it was not until November that the air organization saw fit to create a specialist unit. On 23 November the 1st Groupe de Bombardment (GB1) was formed under Cdt. de Barès, its three squadrons (VB1, VB2, VB3) being equipped with 18 Voisins. Allocated as a strategic asset to Gen. Joffre, the unit undertook its first mission on 12 December when aircraft attacked the railway station at Freiburg. It was still very early days for the strategic air war.

When the First Battle of Ypres opened on 19 October the RFC squadrons, by now concentrated at St Omer, were overstretched as their value for reconnaissance and artillery spotting was now fully appreciated by the land commanders. On 20 November Sir John French's despatch stated: 'The work performed by the RFC has continued to prove of the utmost value to the success of the operations. The development of their use and employment has indeed been quite extraordinary, and I feel that no effort should be spared to increase their numbers and perfect their equipment and efficiency.'

While the tactical employment of aircraft was receiving plaudits, the strategic use received another boost on 21 November with a spectacular raid on the Zeppelin factory at Friedrichshafen. The attack was made by a special RNAS unit equipped with Avro 504As that had deployed to Belfort especially for this long-range mission. Three of the four aircraft ('873, '874 and '875) took off successfully at about 9.30am and flew the zigzag route to the target, arriving overhead around midday. Bombs were dropped on various targets causing a fair degree of damage; Flt. Lt. S.V. Sippe and Flt. Cdr. J.T. Babbington returned safely but Sq. Cdr. E. Featherstone-Briggs was shot down and taken prisoner.

The RNAS continued to develop its strategic vision with a plan to attack the airship sheds at Cuxhaven–Nordholz. On 25 December 1914 an attack force comprising the three seaplane carriers plus escort arrived off Heligoland in the early hours of the morning. Seven aircraft launched just after 7am and made their way towards the target; 30 minutes later the fleet was attacked by German airships and aircraft but without any damage being caused. Meanwhile, fog over the target had meant an aborted mission and the seaplanes tried to return to their fleet, all but two were safely recovered – although in the meantime the fleet had once more come under air attack.

It was also in December that the Russians formed a specialist bomber squadron – but at private expense when Sikorskii was given authority to undertake an 'operational trial' with his Ilya Muromets bombers. Two of these mammoth aircraft had been available since August but had seen little employment in the face of disinterest and even scepticism; this had even led to cancellation of an order for 32 more aircraft and it was at that point that Sikorskii made his offer. The Flying Ship Squadron was duly formed and was ready for operations at the turn of the year.

The aeroplane had gone to war in August 1914 with few supporters and little real idea of what it could (or could not) do. A great many army commanders were unwilling to place any reliance on the new machines, but over a period of months, as the benefits of aerial reconnaissance and artillery spotting in particular became evident, then the calls for air support became ever more urgent. Gen. Iurii Danilov reported:

> as a consequence of our lack of sufficient aeroplanes, the enemy could manoeuvre as he wished by using his highly developed rail network and be certain that his plans would not be discovered by us very quickly. At the same time, with considerably better aviation facilities, the enemy was able to observe each of our steps with complete impunity.

The pre-war organisation was woefully inadequate in all areas and changes had to be made without the benefit of any overall planning. It was late in the year, for example, before most Command HQs had any type of 'air adviser'. The supply of replacement aircraft was nothing short of a shambles in most cases, although the RFC appears to have had the best system with its 'air parks'. The German example was perhaps the worst, with front-line units sending pilots back to aircraft manufacturers to obtain whatever aircraft they could and with

higher command having no real idea what was going on. None of the major combatants had an aircraft or aero engine manufacturing organization that was able to cope with the ever-increasing demands for equipment to replace losses never mind to create new units. In Germany the situation was made worse by political wrangling between the Prussian and Bavarian war ministries.

The initial French concept was one of not ordering more aircraft, and even shutting down training schools to get the maximum strength at the front for the expected 'short war'. However, as early as October, the French had in fact put forward a proposal for a major development of military aviation with a plan to more than double the number of squadrons at the front to 65 (with almost 400 aircraft) within three months and to give them specialized roles; these latter were specified as Bomber (16 squadrons of Voisins with 130hp Salmson engines), Reconnaissance/Fighter (16 squadrons of Morane-Saulniers with 80hp Le Rhône), Observation (30 squadrons of Morane-Saulniers with 80hp Renault or Caudrons with 80hp Le Rhône) and Cavalry (3 squadrons). It was a bold and forward-looking plan and at about the same time a new Director of Military Aviation, Gen. Hirschaur, was appointed with a remit to streamline the production and delivery of aircraft and engines. In practice it was to prove far more difficult to execute.

The RFC units in France were re-organized a number of times in the latter part of the year to reflect changes in Army organization. By 25 December 1st Wing (2 Squadron and 3 Squadron) supported Haig's 1st Army and 2nd Wing (5 Squadron and 6 Squadron) supported Smith-Dorrien's 2nd Army, with four further squadrons based with HQ RFC at St Omer.

At this time the German Air Service was not particularly active on the Western Front although – like the RFC and the French Air Service – it was engaged on regular reconnaissance and artillery co-operation work. Indeed, other than the strategic bombing doctrine implemented from 1915, the German Air Service in general had a defensive doctrine that was to last throughout the war. Prior to the outbreak of war, the Airship Battalion, with whom air matters rested, had drawn up the requirements for an aeroplane: 'the flying machine must always be able to carry two people, only one of whom is required to operate the apparatus. The second is entrusted solely with undertaking a military task.'

This military task was, in common with practice in other nations, seen as being primarily that of reconnaissance. However, it was recognized by some individuals that combat between aeroplanes would become inevitable. Maj. Siegert of the General Staff later wrote:

> it will not be possible to operate without weapons. Every reconnaissance flight will result in an encounter with enemy aircraft . . . it is likely that an aircraft which is capable of shooting at an enemy machine will have the advantage. The most suitable weapon is a light, air-cooled machine-gun . . . it is essential that aircraft are designed which permit the use of weapons in the widest possible sector, above, below and to both sides.

As early as January 1913 Franz Schneider had registered a patent for a gun firing through a hollow propeller shaft, an idea that was adopted by Second World War German fighters such as the Bf 109. Despite such forward thinking, little came of this until almost two years of war had passed. Despite this, development of the capability to combat other aircraft in the air was slow – largely due to the limitations of the aircraft types in service and a perception that combat would detract from the primary, army support role of the aircraft. Most developments were left to individual pilots or units. In late September 1914 two single-seat Bristol Scouts had joined the RFC in France, one going to 3 Squadron and one to 5 Squadron. Both aircraft were fitted with rifles fixed to fire outside the propeller arc. The first confirmed Allied air-to-air success went to Sgt. Joseph Frantz and Cap. Quénault in a Voisin of VB24 when they used a Hotchkiss machine gun to shoot down an Aviatik near Reims on 5 October.

Nonetheless, it was very much a matter of individual choice as to what armament, if any, to take into the air. Most crews took revolvers, so that if they forced down an enemy aircraft they could land alongside and take their opponents prisoner – or defend themselves if they were forced down. Indeed, although some chose to fit machine guns this was often in direct contravention of squadron orders! There were other more drastic ways to bring down the enemy – on 9 September the commander of the Russian 11th Corps Air Unit, Pyotr Nesterov, was so determined that the German Albatros that was attacking his base should not escape that he rammed and destroyed his opponent. He was declared a hero; a tradition that was to continue into the days of the Soviet Air Force when ramming enemy aircraft was considered to be a good technique. Meanwhile, also in Russia, it was announced that volunteer pilots – male or female – would be welcome as long as they brought their own aircraft!

Although this account will not cover the war in the Far East between Japan and Germany, as very little air action took place there, it is worth noting the mission of 5 September when two Japanese aircraft attacked German shipping and sank a torpedo boat – the first such success by an aircraft against a naval vessel.

Air Power Comes of Age

From the early uncertain beginnings, the impact of the aeroplane on the war was to be of increasing importance during 1915; a reflection of this new-found importance was the perceived need to deny the airspace over one's own lines to the enemy – and so the fighter was born. It was also the year in which the theatre of war widened to include Africa and the Middle East.

Aerial reconnaissance remained of paramount importance and with the now static nature of trench warfare the prime requirement was for aerial photographs. In January 1915 the RFC had an experimental photographic section, under Lt. J. Moore-Brabazon, operating with the 1st Wing. Part of their task was to develop a practical aerial camera and by March the first examples of the 'A' camera (designed in conjunction with the Thornton-Pickard Manufacturing Company) were in operational use. The success of this system led to the formation of photographic sections with the other RFC Wings. The value of such aerial photography was immediately apparent: the attack plan used by the British First Army at Neuve Chapelle for the offensive launched on 10 March was based upon such work. The village was captured within four hours, although the offensive was then held up by a number of strongpoints.

The number of aircraft involved in any action was still very small but they were increasingly used to increase the offensive power of the main battlefield weapon – massed artillery. One vital aspect of this was counter-battery fire and a great deal of air effort was expended on this task. Air power was also employed in a strategic sense during this battle, with aircraft being sent to attack rail communications in an effort to stem the flow of German reinforcements to the battle area.

Rail Targets

The crucial role played by rail communications in the mobility of armies during the First World War cannot be over-emphasized; Gen. Ludendorff later wrote: 'experience has taught us that a modern army cannot operate more than 120km from its railheads.' With the excellent rail infrastructure in most of Europe, commanders had come to rely on rail as the means of rapid and mass transportation. Before the advent of air power there was no real threat to the security of such installations 'behind the lines'.

The first such attack was by Capt. G. Carmichael of 5 Squadron who dropped a 100lb (45kg) bomb on the rail line at Mersin during the afternoon of 10 March, the opening day of the Battle of Neuve Chapelle. Other aircraft attacked Courtrai, Lille, Douai and Don. This was also the first time that a concerted effort was made to obtain a photographic mosaic of the enemy trench lines – 2 Squadron and 3 Squadron carrying out this task. The third role, artillery co-operation, was equally important and numerous sorties were flown, especially for counter-battery work. On the night of 11 March, three BE2bs of 4 Squadron were deployed to bomb the railway junction near Lille, the first such night bombing venture by the RFC. At around the same time, the German Air Service was beginning to introduce its new C-types, more powerful aircraft that were often armed with machine guns.

On 22 April the Germans launched an offensive at Ypres, which included the first use of gas as a precursor to the attack. Once again, RFC attacks on rail facilities were a significant part of the air effort and on one such sortie the first Victoria Cross to be awarded for an air action was won. Lt. William Rhodes-Moorhouse of 2 Squadron left Merville in BE2b '687 with its single 100lb (45kg) bomb at 3.50pm on 22 April to attack Courtrai. He arrived at the target and flew over the area at 300ft (90m) in order to ensure the accuracy of his bombing. His aircraft was immediately raked with ground fire and he was seriously wounded; nevertheless he flew back to his base and despite his wounds and loss of blood insisted on delivering his report. He died the following day. This was the first of 19 air VCs awarded during the First World War.

The British offensive at Aubers Ridge, launched on 9 May, brought another role to the RFC's aircraft: the contact patrol. One of the first units to be engaged in this work was 16 Squadron and their basic task was to keep track of Allied soldiers and report their positions back to HQ. At first, this was facilitated by the soldiers carrying with them strips of white cloth to lay down as identification panels; later techniques involved soldiers wearing reflective metal triangles on their backpacks, which would glint in the sun and reveal their position. While this was of course valuable in helping to clear the fog of war, it was not covert and the enemy could equally well observe the signals.

In the early part of 1915, the French GHQ had been pressing for an effective bomber that could be used to attack Germany and the War Ministry offered incentives for such designs; the January air plan called for 21 new bombing squadrons. In the meantime, GB1 was using Voisins and attacking targets by throwing modified 90mm artillery shells over the side of the aircraft, although bomb racks were subsequently designed to carry 40kg (88lb) bombs, which were modified 155mm shells. Under the influence of Cdt. Barès, GB1 carried out intensive training and planning for its strategic role and Barès produced a list of targets that he considered appropriate – this being approved by Joffre in January. Following the German use of poison gas at Ypres in April, it was decided to attack the BASF (Badische Anilin und Soda Fabrik) gas works at Ludwigshafen and GB1 modified its Voisins to carry larger fuel tanks as part of the detailed planning for this raid.

Eighteen bombers left Malzeville in the early hours of 27 May and arrived over the target at around 6am, where they proceeded to drop 87 bombs and cause a moderate amount of damage. The raid leader, De Goys, had technical trouble and was taken prisoner when he force-landed near the target. The interest in a bomber force was confirmed in June with a GHQ plan for 50 squadrons, each of 10 aircraft, with the intention to attack industrial targets in the Ruhr; however, there was still no suitable aircraft design to put into mass production.

Meanwhile, three other bombing groups had been formed (GB2 in January, GB3 in March and GB4 in May) and by July all were concentrated at Malzeville in what was an impressive array of strategic air power – albeit still equipped with Voisins. They flew a number of bombing missions, the largest of which was on 25 August when 62 bombers attacked the steelworks and blast furnaces at Dillingen. Fifty bombers reached the target, the others either returning with technical problems or failing to find the target, and all but one returned safely.

GHQ was now calling for a bomber force of 1,000 aircraft to win the war by attacking military-industrial targets and lines of communication. However, absence of suitable designs and pressure for other aircraft types and roles led to a re-think and by November the air plan (for spring 1916) had reduced the bomber quota to a mere 310 aircraft. The air arm was under tight army control and doctrine tied it to the ground operations. Despite its success and the obvious potential of the concept, the French strategic bombing organization was dispersed in the autumn.

The Imperial Russian Air Service, which had been re-organized in January with a unified aviation command under Grand Duke Alexander Mikhailovich, was also active in the strategic bombing role, and the EVK flew its first operation with its Ilya Muromets Type Bs on 15 February when Capt. Gurshkov carried out a long-range mission in his aircraft *Kievsky*.

By the summer of 1915 the value of these operations was widely appreciated and the unit was attacking a variety of targets on the Eastern Front and in East Prussia, with further variants of the Ilya Muromets entering service during the year. They were also employed on long-range reconnaissance missions, such as on 31 March when an aircraft flew a route of almost 340 miles (550km) to monitor German troop movements. They proved remarkably effective despite their somewhat cumbersome appearance and with their heavy armament were able to defend themselves against enemy fighters – albeit the latter were neither numerous nor particularly active.

The first Russian fighter aircraft designs came to fruition in 1915, with the RBVZ-16 from the Russian Baltic Company, followed by the armoured RBVZ-17 and, later in the year, the experimental Lebed IX and XII.

The war widened when Italy declared war on Austria–Hungary on 23 May. The following day Austrian Taubes attacked the naval arsenal at Venice – four bombs dropped on the city and seven others in the bay and lagoon. The Austrians were forced

to reduce the scale of their previous operations on the Eastern and Balkan Fronts and concentrate on this new threat on the south-west sector; air units were moved into landing grounds in the Alps and Balkans and the air arm was expanded to 18 'flight companies' (Fliegerkompanien).

While most of the activity took place over land, Austrian Lohner flying boats were active over the Adriatic. The Italians had been among the first to develop the military use of aircraft, employing them on colonial operations from 1910. At the declaration of war the Air Service had 150 operational aircraft, mainly of French origin, while naval aviation had only 19 seaplanes and six airships. Although development was slow it was significant – including deployment from August 1915 of one of the earliest purpose-built bombers, the Caproni Ca1.

However, the Western Front remained the most active in terms of air power. In a report on 15 June the BEF Commander-in-Chief stated that 'the RFC is becoming more and more an indispensable factor in combined operations . . . in spite of the opposition of hostile aircraft and the great number of anti-aircraft guns employed by the enemy, air reconnaissance has been carried out with regularity and accuracy.'

The need for an aircraft designed for air to air fighting was given the attention that was long overdue and the first dedicated fighters appeared in the spring of 1915 in the shape of the Vickers FB.5. The first RFC unit to have these was 5 Squadron, and they replaced its Voisins and Martinsydes starting in March while the unit was based at Bailleul.

The first FB.5s had been delivered at the beginning of the year but had not been concentrated with a single unit; furthermore it was not until the arrival of 11 Squadron in July that a fully equipped and operational FB.5 unit was available. Typical of the engagements of the period was that of 10 May, when 2nd Lt. W. Acland (with observer/gunner Airman Rogers) in 5 Squadron Vickers FB.5 '1616 reported:

I patrolled the Ypres salient. We sighted an aeroplane not being shelled about 3 to 4 miles away to the SE and high up. We climbed to about 10,000ft and gave chase. We caught him up and opened fire from above and behind at about 50 yards. The pilot was hit, and the machine also, as I saw flakes of material flying off. They dived and we followed, and the observer fired with his pistol, but did little damage . . . The machine nose-dived from about 1500ft, turned on her back and fell to the ground quite near to Lille.

The FB.5 was in fact no real surprise to the Germans as aircraft '621 had, on 28 February, been captured intact when forced to land, both crewmen being taken prisoner.

There was a notable success on 7 June when Flt. Sub. Lt. Reginald Warneford scored the first aerial success against an airship, bringing down the LZ-37 near Ostend. For this remarkable achievement he was awarded the VC. The award of another VC – to Capt. Lanoe Hawker of 6 Squadron – followed an air combat on 25 July during which he had, in his Bristol Scout, shot down two enemy aircraft and forced a third down out of control. This was indeed confirmation that air fighting had come of age and was now a deadly pursuit.

French Fighter Squadrons

The French Air Service formed its first three fighter squadrons in late spring: MS3, MS12 and MS23. These were all equipped, as their nomenclature shows, with the Morane-Saulnier monoplane. However, individualism still reigned and Roland Garros, with his mechanic Jules Hue, devised a simple system of enabling an 8mm Hotchkiss machine gun to be mounted above the engine so that it could fire straight ahead, making aiming easy. His system involved nothing more complex than fitting metal plates on the rear faces of the propeller blades so that any bullets that did not pass between the blades would strike the plates and be deflected.

By the spring of 1915 Garros was ready to give the system an operational test and in the first few weeks of April managed to shoot down three German aircraft. His success was short-lived as on 19 April he was forced to land behind enemy lines, providing the Germans with the secret of his gun.

German Successes

The following month saw the Germans testing out similar fittings but there was apparently no urgency to the trials, despite the need to combat the success of French fighters such as the excellent Morane-Saulnier monoplane. However, Fokker had combined the new gun system into their E.1 Eindecker and it was this that was to be the next major advance in the story of aerial warfare.

Reports of a new type of enemy fighter had been included in RFC communiqués in July, for example: 'On July 26, near Roulers, Lt. Bell Irving in a Bristol Scout of 1 Squadron, was attacked by a German machine, which had the appearance of a very small LVG. It was armed with a machine gun.' Such reports increased in frequency through the summer as each side attempted to prevent reconnaissance sorties being flown.

On 26 August it was reported that

Lt. Greenwood and Capt. Lombridge in a BE2c, while engaged in taking photos over Hanbourdin, were attacked by a German machine that approached from behind and dived underneath them, opening fire with a machine gun from below. It then circled round and behind, evidently to fit a new drum to the machine gun . . . the hostile machine returned to the fight and passed across the left bow, evidently thinking that our gun could only be fired from the rear mounting, but the observer had in the meantime changed the gun to the front mounting and so was able to keep the hostile machine under fire until it flew away.

Such inconclusive combats remained the norm, but the need to develop an effective air fighting capability was now fully appreciated, and late 1915 was to see a marked change in the nature of the air war as both sides fought to achieve air superiority by driving their enemies from the air. On 1 August, Max Immelmann of FAb62 scored his first victory with the new Fokker E1 Eindecker, shooting down 2nd Lt. Reid in BE2c '1662 of 2 Squadron near Douai. It was one of only two such aircraft with the unit at this time as deliveries were slow. Airborne in the other Fokker was Oswald Boelcke but on this occasion he was out of luck as his gun jammed; however, he was enthusiastic about the aircraft: 'With the single-seater my ideal is achieved; now I can be pilot, observer and fighter all at the same time.' From now on these two outstanding German fighter pilots frequently flew as a hunting pair.

The initial German concept was to provide one or two of the new fighters to each unit rather than put them together as specialist units – that would come later after individual pilots had shown the worth of the type and developed a tactical awareness of how best to use the fighters. Although the RFC did not yet know it, the 'Fokker Scourge' was starting.

The RFC also had a new fighter appearing this summer, the first DH2 being with 5

Squadron for evaluation in July. Unfortunately this DH2 ('4732) was damaged and forced to land behind enemy lines on 9 August, presenting the Germans with an example of the latest British fighter. Although the type had been ordered into production it would be 1916 before it became truly operational on the Western Front.

Attack on England

July 1915 saw the Kaiser agree to unrestricted airship attacks on England. A number of raids had been launched in the first half of 1915, but there was a prohibition against attacking London (although from April onwards certain outlying parts of the city had been included on the target list).

Indeed, the first airship attack on England had taken place on 19 January when L-3 and L-4 bombed targets in East Anglia, the most serious damage being caused at Kings Lynn where four people were killed. Further raids had followed and on 31 May London was hit for the first time. The public outcry was intense – Britain itself was under attack. The responsibility for home defence against aerial attack rested with the Admiralty who employed a small number of aircraft at various coastal stations. These were woefully inadequate in terms of performance, and there was no kind of air warning system.

In October the RFC was tasked to bring machines 'to the vicinity of London' for a trial period of anti-airship operations – as much a political move as a military one at this stage. Seven BE2cs and one SE4a were deployed to landing grounds around London and after the trial period from 4 to 12 October their presence was extended to 'an indefinite period'. There was only one major raid after this; five airships attacked London on the night of 13/14 October, causing 71 casualties and £80,000 worth of damage. This was the largest casualty list to date and the six sorties mounted by the RFC were all to no avail.

The Zeppelins ruled the night skies over England and were becoming more effective. The winter weather brought an end to their attacks for 1915 but it was certain that they would return in 1916 in greater numbers. The Home Defence organization was in drastic need of improvement in terms of equipment and tactics but as far as aeroplanes were concerned the Western Front

was screaming out for everything that could be provided.

Autumn in Flanders

Haig's 1st Army launched its offensive (the Battle of Loos) on 25 September with air power an integral part of the plan, primarily for reconnaissance and for the interdiction of rail communications on the Lille–Valenciennes–Douai line, plus the bombing of selected munitions sites such as Mons and Namur. Typical of the rail attacks was when 'The line Douai–Valenciennes was bombed by 111th Wing. A truck on the railway was hit from a height of 500ft by a bomb dropped by Lt. Horsfall of 4 Squadron and the line was damaged in several places. A junction was hit by one 100lb bomb and four 20lb bombs dropped from a height of 150ft by Lt. Nicholls, the rails and turntable were probably damaged.'

While at this stage the weight of bombs being dropped – especially when compared to the weight of an average artillery bombardment – appears almost insignificant, they nonetheless proved effective in material and morale terms. Some 92 such attacks were made from 23 to 28 September, eliciting praise from the land commander, who wrote 'especially to thank pilots and observers for their plucky work in co-operating with the artillery, in photography and observation and the bombing attacks on the enemy railways, which were of great value in interrupting his communications.'

Autumn 1915 also saw the introduction of new aircraft, including the Nieuport 11 Bébé, the first of what was to become a string of successful fighter designs from this company. Its overall good performance was somewhat marred by the poor armament but the aircraft was good enough to match and out-perform the Fokkers by the time sufficient numbers had reached the frontline. The first operational aircraft were sent to N65 and employed on air defence of the Nancy area.

Reconnaissance – and the destruction of the enemy reconnaissance capability – remained the most important task. This included the destruction of kite balloons, attacks on which are frequently recorded although they were dangerous targets to attack as they were invariably defended by anti-aircraft guns. A typical attack was that reported by the RFC on 10 September: 'Aeroplanes of IInd Wing, in conjunction with the artillery of IInd Army, attacked

German kite balloons. At a pre-arranged time the field artillery fired on known anti-aircraft guns while the aeroplanes attacked the balloons. When they were hauled down, heavy artillery shelled the balloons on the ground, being ranged by wireless from aeroplanes.'

From 21 to 24 September aircraft co-operated with artillery in the pre-offensive barrage for the British attack at Loos. There was also a co-ordinated bombing campaign and a scheme of protective patrols. Once the battle had started, contact patrols were of critical importance. By October the still small number of Fokker fighters had become a serious problem for the Allies; with effective tactics the German pilots had established a morale superiority that far outweighed their actual numbers. Thus the RFC perceived an increasing need to escort all sorties.

The increasing use of aircraft and their impact made them targets on the ground as well as in the air and from summer 1915 onwards there are increased references to attacks on enemy aerodromes. Typical of these early raids was that of 11 November: 'Six machines of 7 Squadron, each carrying two 100lb bombs, attacked the aerodrome at Gits at 2 p.m. No sheds received an actual hit, two bombs fell about 100 yards away, the remainder falling on or near the aerodrome.'

Other attacks were planned on a larger scale, such as the raid of 11 November on Bellenglise:

An attempt was made by machines of IIIrd Wing to bomb the aerodrome at Bellinglise, about 26 miles east of Albert. The intention was for 4, 8 and 13 Squadrons to send all available aeroplanes to attack the aerodrome simultaneously, each squadron providing its own escort. Half the machines carried a passenger and a half load of bombs, the remaining machines without passengers a full load of bombs. No 11 Squadron patrolled the areas lying between Péronne and St Quentin to prevent interference by any hostile machines.

In the event, poor weather interfered with elements of the plan to make it less effective than hoped; two BE2cs of 8 Squadron were shot down.

Other Theatres

In 1915 the war had extended to areas outside Europe – but in the air the major involvement remained the Western Front,

and these other operations are given only passing mention here.

The Allied decision to try and force Turkey out of the war by striking at the Dardanelles was a bold strategy that was to end in disaster. Spotting for naval gunfire was a major role for aircraft deployed with the fleet in the Dardanelles campaign, as was reconnaissance – the latter including the monitoring of minefields at a time when the Navy still hoped to force their way through the Narrows. Air strength was reinforced with the arrival of additional land-based RNAS units; 3 Squadron RNAS, for example, moved to Tenedos in March. The Gallipoli landings began on 25 April and the few aircraft available were kept very busy.

Poor leadership in the land campaign led to many wasted opportunities and the air assets were always overworked, even after the arrival of No. 2 Wing in August. Long-range interdiction missions were flown against the Berlin to Constantinople (now Istanbul) railway as well as a variety of other targets. Perhaps the most significant event for air power took place on 12 August when Flt. Cdr. C. Edmonds used a 14in torpedo to sink a Turkish ship. Flying a Short 184 seaplane from the Ben-my-Chree, Edmonds hit a 5,000-ton supply ship. He repeated the success on 17 August by hitting a transport ship. However, despite such promise for the new weapon, little real development was carried out during the next few years. Minefields were one of the main tactics employed in naval warfare and the Turks had sown large numbers of mines in and around the Bosporus. Aircraft were used to plot the development of the minefields and to seek clear channels – especially prior to the attempt by Allied warships to force a passage.

April saw the small South African Aviation Unit – comprising three all-steel Henri-Farmans and two BE2cs – join the Expeditionary Force bound for German South West Africa (now Namibia). By early May they were operating from Omaruru on reconnaissance and the bombing of enemy camps. The German colony capitulated on 9 July and the unit was disbanded.

Minor operations also took place around German East Africa (now part of Tanzania) although these were directly connected with the search for and destruction of the cruiser Königsberg. By February a seaplane unit was operating from Niororo Island to track the ship; offensive action had to await the arrival of a pair of Monitors in June.

The end came on 11 July when, using air spotting, the German cruiser was reduced to a blazing wreck. The RNAS seaplane unit subsequently moved to Mombasa.

In Egypt the previous November, a detachment of the Indian Central Flying School had arrived at Alexandria tasked with the air defence of the Suez canal. By early 1915 the unit had eight aircraft, mainly Farmans, but was assisted in its task by a detachment of seven French seaplanes from the seaplane carrier Aénne Rickmers. Operations remained on a small scale throughout 1915 as procedures were developed for co-operation with ground forces such as the Camel Corps, and a number of landing grounds were established. An attempted Turkish offensive in February was easily repulsed and the aircraft flew both reconnaissance and bombing missions. The increased air requirement meant that by November HQ 5th Wing had been established with 14 Squadron, 17 Squadron and 'X' Aircraft park for duties in Egypt.

In Mesopotamia (now mainly Iraq) the first use of aircraft was during the Battle of Qurna at the end of May when two Farmans detached from Egypt flew reconnaissance missions from their base at Basra and a number of advanced landing grounds. By August this unit had been designated as 'A' Flight 30 Squadron and additional aircraft arrived, operating in conjunction with occasional RNAS detachments of Short seaplanes. The reconnaissance, and some bombing missions, continued throughout the year and proved invaluable – though they were often difficult over the vast, featureless landscape of this theatre.

There is insufficient space to mention the training aspects of the various air arms other than in passing, but it is necessary to appreciate the importance and scale of these activities. As front-line strength expanded, the training organizations had to grow to meet the requirements; this needed not only infrastructure such as landing grounds and buildings but also a large number of aircraft and pilots. By the end of 1915 the German Air Service was operating 20 flying schools plus four specializing in observer training, and even the French had started to increase their training organization. As new types of aircraft entered service, redundant types were sent to the training schools.

Despite continued problems in almost all countries with production of aircraft and aero engines, there was also an expansion of production capacity with numerous licence-build agreements.

Conclusions on 1915

The Germans ended 1915 with still an essentially defensive strategy and mentality, save for the strategic bombing by airships, although morale had greatly improved and the Air Service had begun to develop into an effective fighting arm.

The RFC and the French Air Service had a very mixed year with general expansion and the introduction of new types but with a broadly unchanged doctrine based on the need of the army for air reconnaissance and artillery support. The Germans had introduced true strategic bombing with their attacks on London, giving the British an additional air power problem to resolve. Air combat had begun in earnest but many lessons had still painfully to be learned.

Operations away from the Western Front were still generally on a small scale but the scene was set for the air war to expand in 1916 and take on increasing importance in the general conduct of military operations.

Above: **The basic nature of aeroplane design is evident in this Bristol Boxkite. The first powered aeroplane flight had taken place in 1903 but in the absence of military interest (and therefore investment) development was slow and left to private venture.** (Ken Delve Collection)

Left: **It was a similar story in most countries and the similarity of the above design and this from Aviatik AG in Germany is obvious.** (MAP)

Right: **The de Havilland Army aeroplane' as this Royal Aircraft Factory FE.1 (for Farman Experimental) is titled on this photograph was the first product of Geoffrey de Havilland, a pusher type with a 45hp engine that he sold to the Government and that became the first aircraft from the new Royal Aircraft Factory. In 1911 it had passed its acceptance by flying for 'one hour without adjustment or repair'.**

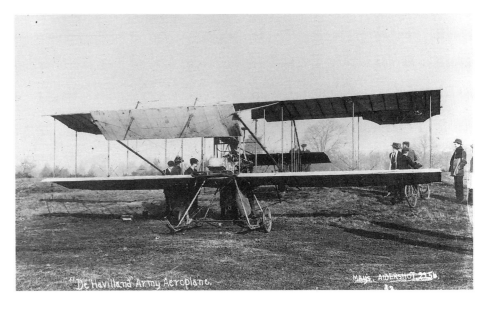

Above: **Workshops at the Central Flying School, one of the elements established when the British created their military air arms in 1912. The rudder to the right shows aircraft 412, a Henri-Farman (formerly serial No 208), one of two Henri-Farmans acquired by the Royal Flying Corps when it formed in 1912. Like so many of the early aeroplanes used by European nations these were of French manufacture.** (Ken Delve Collection)

Centre: **Another of the common French designs in this early period was the Deperdussin series of monoplanes from the Armand Deperdussin works in France and its British counterpart. These tractor type monoplanes, however, acquired a poor reputation with a number of fatal crashes – the net result of which was, for the British, a ban on monoplane designs.** (Peter Green Collection)

Below: **The 'bird-like' origins of some of the early designs can clearly be seen in the wing design of the Handley Page 'Yellow Peril'. No type of this design entered service with the British military because of the monoplane ban.** (*FlyPast* Collection)

Right: A number of aircraft designs were acquired and tested in the period from 1912 to 1914. One such under British test – the Royal Naval Air Service having an interest in seaplane types – was the Borel monoplane seaplane, which was taken on strength at Calshot in July 1913 and flown by Sub. Lt. J.L. Travers (as serial '83). It was kept on strength until late the following year. (Peter Green Collection)

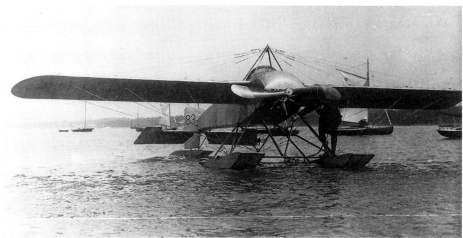

Left: There was enormous resistance in many influential military circles to the creation of 'flying services' and a determination that they should be kept subservient to land force requirements. It took a number of major Army manoeuvres to demonstrate the value of aerial reconnaissance to the land force commanders. Here, one of the RFC's first aircraft makes the first flypast at a Salisbury Plain exercise. (Ken Delve Collection)

Left: This photograph depicts a famous pre-war event when Capt. Charles Longcroft of 2 Squadron, RFC flew a record-breaking trip in BE2a '218. In August 1913 he flew from Farnborough to Montrose in 7 hours 40 minutes with only one stop. Endurance and reliability were key elements for the reconnaissance role. (Peter Green Collection)

Right: On 1 February 1912 Geoffrey de Havilland made the first flight in what was to become the first truly successful British military aeroplane – the Royal Aircraft Factory's BE2 (for Blériot Experimental). It had already been decided that a useful military aeroplane needed two seats – one for the pilot and one for an observer to carry out the actual aerial observation. The basic requirements of such an aircraft were for stability and endurance and the BE2 achieved both of these. (Ken Delve Collection)

Below: The BE2, powered by a 60 or 70hp Renault engine – French aero engines were to remain among the best designs throughout the war – carried out a number of military trials, even at one stage being fitted with floats for seaplane tests, and was ordered into production with various British aircraft companies. With its maximum speed of 70mph (110kph) and ceiling of 10,000ft (3,000m) it was on a par with the designs being developed in France and Germany. (Harry Holmes)

Left: The Royal Aircraft Factory's role included all aspects of aeroplane design and their operational employment; this trials role was to be of great importance to British military development. Here, BE2a '601 is undergoing investigations into aircraft stability, hence the two small fins on the upper wing. (Harry Holmes)

Below: The BE2c was the definitive version of the BE2 series by the outbreak of war; it was a type that saw distinguished service in the early months. This example is seen with 2 Squadron at Netheravon in June 1914. (Ken Delve Collection)

Above: Line-up of BE2 early variants at the CFS at Upavon in 1914 (note that '416 is a BE6). The type proved to be not only a useful operational aeroplane but also a very effective trainer type. (Ken Delve Collection)

Centre left: While the BE2 was the main tractor type in British service, the Farmans were the prime pusher types, as shown here in this line up of Henri-Farmans including '274, '351, and '708 (with BE2s in the background). The advantage with this design was that the observer in the nose had an exceptional all-round view. (Ken Delve Collection)

Below: The other Farman variant was the Maurice-Farman, shown here in the S.11 Shorthorn version with 2 Squadron RNAS. Maximum speed was only 72mph (116kph) but endurance was almost four hours and the type was, despite its appearance, fairly rugged. (Peter Green Collection)

Left: **Maurice-Farman Longhorn N5729, one of a batch of 30 built by the Brush Electrical Engineering Company, with an 80hp Renault engine. Like most of the Farmans, this type served primarily as a trainer and remained in use until 1918.** (Peter Green Collection)

Right: **Although the Maurice-Farmans, this being an S.7 Longhorn variant, were on operational strength in mid 1914 they saw only limited operational service; a number were given machine gun armament as part of early trials into such weapons on aircraft. The tractor design meant that such a weapon could be satisfactorily mounted at the front but the additional weight reduced the already barely adequate performance.** (Peter Green Collection)

Left: **BE2c '2026 of 12 Squadron, RFC. This was one of a number of units to use the type operationally on the Western Front – indeed, a BE2c of 2 Squadron was the first British aeroplane to land in France when the RFC deployed in support of the British Expeditionary Force.** (Capt. D.S. Glover)

Right: The BE2c Squadrons proved invaluable in the early months of the war, providing timely reconnaissance to the commanders on the ground. Furthermore, it was not long before they were showing their value in co-operating with the artillery on spotting fall of shot; this particular role, in which the RFC squadrons became particularly adept, grew in importance as the land battle became more static. (Ken Delve Collection)

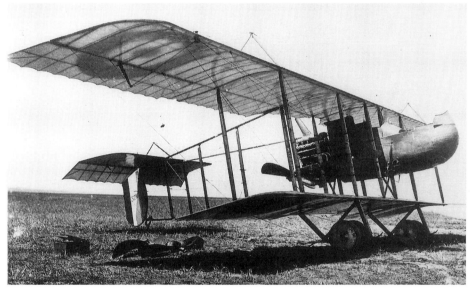

Left: One of the major problems for all the air forces was that of ground fire – and the fact that troops tried to shoot at any and every aeroplane! National markings were painted on aircraft to show ground and air forces whose side you were on. The British at first adopted a Union Flag but as the central cross element was mistaken for the cross used by the Germans, they soon decided to adopt a roundel similar to that used by the French but with reversed colours (the red in the centre). This Maurice-Farman Shorthorn clearly shows a roundel on the upper wing – note also how transparent the fabric is. (Peter Green Collection)

Right: The RNAS were concerned by the threat of the German airships to naval operations and adopted an offensive strategy of attacking them in their sheds. Flying a Sopwith Tabloid ('168 and not '394 as shown here) Reggie Marix destroyed Zeppelin Z9 in its shed at Düsseldorf on 8 October 1914. (Peter Green Collection)

Left: One of the many 1913 designs aimed at providing an effective reconnaissance and bomber aircraft. The RE5 was in essence an enlarged version of the RE1 and led to further designs that were somewhat more successful. This particular aircraft has been modified to single seat configuration in order to achieve a number of height records. In June 1914 the commanding officer of 6 Squadron, Maj. J.H.W. Becke, claimed to have reached 19,000ft (5,790m). (Peter Green Collection)

Right: The German Air Service entered the war with a number of types. Most, as with the RFC, were for reconnaissance duties. Among the best was the Aviatik B.1 as shown here. (MAP)

Left: Friedrichshafen developed a superb series of seaplanes during the war. The FF29, as here, was produced from late 1914 for coastal patrol duties. (MAP)

Flieger auf Rumpler-Taube

Above: **A Rumpler Taube. Various companies produced Taube designs, a number of which saw operational service, but it is the Rumpler version that is best remembered.**

Below left: **An Aviatik of 1914. References to Aviatiks occur frequently in RFC reports in the first year of the war.** (Ken Wixey Collection)

Below right: **The Gotha LD2 was in use, in small numbers, from the outbreak of war. Its 100hp Mercedes D1 gave it a top speed of 65mph (105kph) but by late 1914 it had been phased out of front-line service.** (MAP)

25

Left: Deliveries of the Vickers FB5 'Gunbus' began in December 1914, the type starting its operational career with 5 Squadron in early 1915. This was an attempt to provide an aeroplane armed with a machine gun for the Western Front, after it became apparent that aircraft would have to be armed in order to protect themselves and at the same time destroy the enemy. This particular aircraft, '5659, was at Joyce Green. (Capt. D.S. Glover)

Right: The Austrian Air Arm deployed a number of units to join the campaign against Russia; here an Albatros B1 of Fliegerkompanie 1 is at Brzesko in late 1914. (Stach)

Below: Another of the pusher types, the DH1A with its 120hp Beardmore engine was superior to other contemporary fighters, but it did not see service in France. It was used in the Middle East and by the training organization in the Britain. (*FlyPast* Collection)

Above right: The Morane-Saulnier 'parasol' series of monoplanes saw extensive use with the French and British. Here is a line-up of mixed types – probably L and LAs – with 3 Squadron RFC in 1915. Their main tasks remained those of reconnaissance, including photography and artillery spotting. (Ken Delve Collection)

Above left: Martinsyde S.1 Scout '4250. This was one of the first single-seat scout (fighter) types to serve with the RFC and first appeared in early 1915 as air combat was becoming of increasing importance. Armed with a single Lewis gun on the upper wing, the S.1 was used only in small numbers and was not a great success. (Ken Delve Collection)

Below: The top left of this shot shows Hesdigneul aerodrome in France – home to 2 Squadron and others. (2 Squadron records)

Left: FE8 prototype. This type was under consideration, along with the DH2, for the RFC's fighter requirement in mid 1915. An effective fighter type was needed in France as aircraft began to play an increasing part in the war. (Harry Holmes)

Above: The Airco DH2, powered by a Gnome Monosoupape, was the first effective fighter employed by the RFC. With its top speed of 93mph (150kph), reasonable manoeuvrability and single Vickers gun, the DH2 first flew in mid 1915. However, by the time it reached service in any numbers it was already outclassed. (Ken Delve Collection)

Left: DH2 under trial at Farnborough. Some 400 of the type were eventually delivered to the RFC. (Harry Holmes)

Right: **The Blériot XI was built in five principal versions and was in military use from 1910 – equipping a number of French squadrons by the outbreak of War. It also served with the Italian and British (as here) air arms.** (Ken Wixey Collection)

Left: **The RNAS had from the very first days of the war adopted an offensive strategy for their land-based aeroplanes and seaplanes. This bombed-up Short 184 seaplane was a type that entered service in 1915 and remained in use throughout the war.** (*FlyPast* Collection)

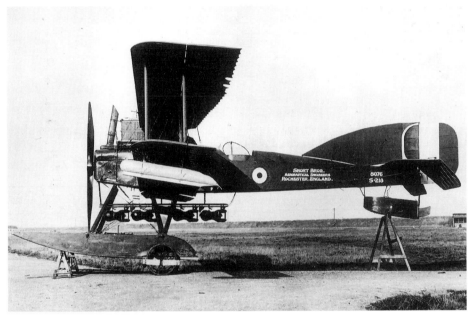

Right: **Some of the first Short 184s went aboard the seaplane carrier *Ben-my-Chree* for the Dardanelles campaign. In August 1915 one of these was used by Flt. Cdr. Edmonds to sink a Turkish ship with a torpedo – the first such success for this weapon when delivered by an aeroplane.** (*FlyPast* Collection)

Left: The French Nieuport company established a reputation for developing a series of fighters that were among the leading designs of the day. This Nieuport 10 ('8517) served with 2 Squadron RNAS and was one of 50 such taken on charge from 1915. (Peter Green Collection)

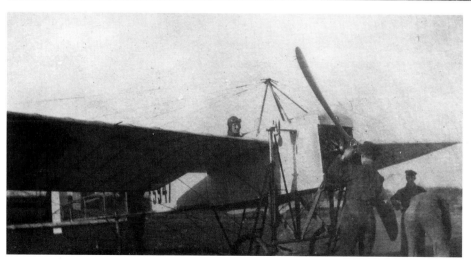

Above: Farman F.40, often known as the Horace Farman, saw limited service with 5 Wing RNAS and was often, as here, armed with Le Prieur rockets on the inter-plane struts. (Ken Delve Collection)

Left: Of the other early designs, the Blériot XI was of particular note and was yet another French type to be used by the British. It was also a long-lived type serving on into 1916 (as with this RNAS example that was delivered in January 1916 by which time they were primarily used for training). (Capt. D.S. Glover)

Right: **While RNAS personnel take to the grass and relax, the cockpit of Bristol TB8 '1216 attracts some attention in this March 1915 scene at Eastchurch. Some 45 landplane versions of this aircraft were used by the RNAS, deliveries commencing in 1914.** (Peter Green Collection)

Left: **The Avro 504 series was another of the great First World War designs with operational and, more especially, training significance. This scene at Baileul in 1915 shows '398 with 5 Squadron.** (Peter Green Collection)

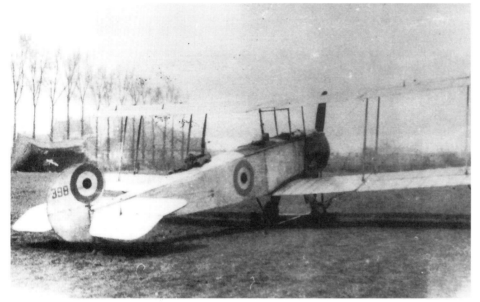

Right: **Allonville and BE2c '1779 of 4 Squadron RFC. The Squadron moved to this airfield in November 1915 and stayed there until February 1916.** (Peter Green Collection)

Left: **Camouflaged Martinsyde S.1 '2449 of 4 Squadron at St Omer in early 1915.** (Peter Green Collection)

Right: **Bristol Scout D '8988. This type, a development of the Scout C, was destined to see extensive operational use in most theatres even though it was never truly successful.** (Peter Green Collection)

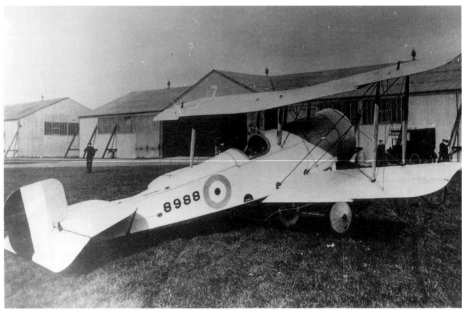

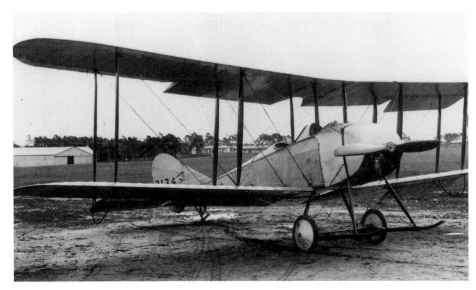

Left: **BE8a '2134 seen at Farnborough. This was a Vickers-built aircraft and after a short period with the Wireless Trials Unit it was allocated to 9 Squadron, which undertook much of this development work. The use of wireless telegraphy was seen as essential, especially for the co-ordination of artillery shoots. The BE8a was often referred to as the 'Bloater' and it saw little operational service.** (Peter Green Collection)

Right: This BE2e, C7001, was also used by the Wireless Experimental Unit and is seen here at Biggin Hill. (Capt. D.S. Glover)

Below: 16 Squadron formed at St Omer in February 1915 during one of the RFC's expansion periods, and was soon heavily engaged on reconnaissance work using a variety of aircraft although, like most units, the BE2c was the main workhorse – indeed, this type remained in service with 16 Squadron until May 1917! (Peter Green Collection)

Above left: **A great many aircraft were forced to land behind enemy lines and often they had little more than engine damage. Here BE2c '2742 is seen with German markings after such an instance.** (Peter Green Collection)

Above right: **The two-seat BE2d had a maximum speed of just over 88mph (142kph) and a ceiling of 12,000ft (3,700m). The pilot sat in the front cockpit, amidst the woodwork of the struts, while the observer sat behind – with a somewhat better field of view. This particular aircraft, '2785, was with CFS at Upavon.** (Peter Green Collection)

Below: **A unique aircraft – the highest serial number issued to a British aircraft and an indication of the rapid increase in aircraft production. The RFC initially numbered its aircraft with three or four digits but when the number 10,000 was reached it had already been decided that the system would be unmanageable. Henceforth, aircraft would carry a serial letter and four numbers, giving far more available combinations. This particular BE2c was a Blackburn-built aircraft.** (Peter Green Collection)

Above left: **Atmospheric shot of the CFS workshops in 1915.**

Above right: **William Rhodes-Moorhouse of 2 Squadron had the distinction of being awarded the first ever Victoria Cross for an aerial action following his bombing attack on Courtrai railway junction in April 1915.** (Peter Green Collection)

Right: **The first French aerial victory went to Joseph Frantz and Louis Quénault of V24 – on 5 October 1914 they were on patrol over Vesle when they spotted an Aviatik, which they promptly attacked. After some 47 rounds, Quénault's Hotchkiss gun jammed – but it had done enough, the German aircraft was in a dive from which it crashed.** (Dennis Hylands)

Below: **Henri-Farman F.16 of the French Air Service powered by an 80hp Gnome engine and used primarily for reconnaissance.** (Ken Delve Collection)

Left: **Morane Parasol of 1914 vintage, the early type with slab-sided fuselage and small tailplane – in German hands.** (Ken Wixey Collection)

Right: **French Morane monoplane with an 80hp Gnome engine. Used by both British and French squadrons, the Morane monoplanes were among the first types to be equipped with a forward-firing machine gun.** (Ken Wixey Collection)

Left: **Caudron G.4 powered by two 80hp Le Rhones.**

36

Left: All the major participants made use of airships, although not on the same scale or with the same strategic vision as the Germans. SS29 was one of the Sea Scout vessels built at Folkestone for the Admiralty for coastal patrol duties looking for submarines; the type was introduced to service in 1915. (Peter Green Collection)

Right: The FF33 was produced in a number of variants and saw extensive use with the German naval air arm for both reconnaissance and fighting from 1915 onwards. Aircraft of this type were also carried on a number of German ships. (MAP)

Below: Albatros Type B at Wilhelmshafen in service with II. Seeflieger Abteilung, probably 1915. The German seaplanes were aggressively operated over the North Sea and carried out a wide range of roles, frequently in conjunction with either submarine or surface vessel operations. (Ken Delve Collection)

37

Left: The Gotha LD.6a was a two-seat long-range reconnaissance type in service from March 1915. In common with most operational types of this period it was also employed as a light bomber with the observer dropping small bombs over the side of the aircraft. (MAP)

Centre left: The Aviatik B.II appeared in limited numbers during 1915 as a two-seat reconnaissance aircraft powered by a 120hp Mercedes DII. Note the identification crosses on the underside of the upper wing and, unusually, on the wheel hubs. (MAP)

Below: Powered by a 160hp Mercedes DIII, the Albatros C.1 was a general purpose aircraft and was one of the most effective types operational in 1915. The photo shows a captured example of the type. (Capt. D.S. Glover)

Right: **The one and only Gotha WD.4, used as a personal aircraft by Capt. Langfeld, commanding officer of the Haltenau naval air station.** (MAP)

Left: **Voisin biplane – used as a reconnaissance aeroplane and for night bombing.** (Ken Wixey Collection)

Right: **The German C-type aeroplanes of 1915 were designed to perform both reconnaissance and escort (limited fighter) roles. It became one of the best-known products of the Automobil und Aviatik Company and was built in appreciable numbers.** (MAP)

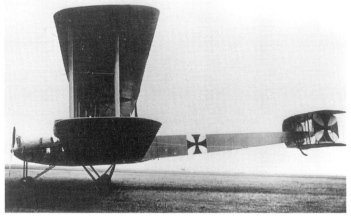

Above left: The Rumpler G.1 went into production in 1915 as a reconnaissance/bomber but only was used in small numbers by the Germans. (MAP)

Above right: Powered by six engines, the Zeppelin-Staaken VGO III was the first of the 'strategic bombers' produced by this company. The aircraft saw operational service with RFa 500 on the Eastern Front in the early days of 1915; although its top speed was only 75mph (120kph) and its ceiling only 6,560ft (2,000m) it was defended by five machine guns. (MAP)

Left: A good illustration of the restricted view of pilots in many of these early designs is given by this LVG C.II. However, this type was one of the first to be armed with a forward-firing Spandau machine gun and a parabellum gun for the observer. The aircraft entered service late in 1915 for a variety of roles. (Heinz Birkholz)

Below: The AGO C.II was designed as a reconnaissance aircraft and appeared in late 1915. The sleek aerodynamic shape and twin-boom configuration made the type quite distinctive. (Ken Delve Collection)

Right: The capture of Garros and his 'gun system' led to the development by Fokker of his series of monoplanes armed with a Spandau firing through the propeller disc using an interrupter gear, in this case an E.III. (Ken Delve Collection)

Below: Another Fokker E.III showing the neat lines of this aircraft and the exceptional field of view for the pilot; one of the criticisms of the design was that the pilot 'sat on top' and was the danger of head injury in the event of the aircraft flipping over in landing. Some 150 of the Oberursel-powered E.IIIs were built and their impact on the air war was far in excess of their actual numbers. This example was captured by the French and subjected to a rigorous technical examination; the results were published in the magazine *L'Aerophile* in 1916. (Ken Delve Collection)

Left: **The Fokker Eindeckers were a favourite mount of Max Immelmann, perhaps the greatest of the early air fighting aces.** (Dennis Hylands)

Right: **The Pfalz E.I had its origins as an unarmed reconnaissance aircraft but with the advent of the Fokker synchronization gear in 1915 it appeared, like the Fokker E.I (and E.III) with a forward-firing Spandau.** (MAP)

Left: **The similarity between the Morane H and the German monoplanes it inspired is obvious in this picture of a captured H. Note the manufacturer's badge on the cowling.** (MAP)

42

Above: The Russian air elements at the outbreak of the war were very weak and relied almost entirely on foreign, particularly French, types. This Maurice-Farman S.11F was in service with the Russian Navy; it was in essence a floatplane version of the Shorthorn with a 70hp Renault engine. (IWM Q64261)

Below: Sikorskii Il-ya Mauromets. The IM name was given to all of Sikorskii's four-engined military aircrtaft, various bomber types of which served throughout the War. (Jack Bruce/Stuart Leslie collection).

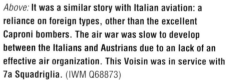

Above: It was a similar story with Italian aviation: a reliance on foreign types, other than the excellent Caproni bombers. The air war was slow to develop between the Italians and Austrians due to an lack of an effective air organization. This Voisin was in service with 7a Squadriglia. (IWM Q68873)

Left: The Austro-Hungarian units were a little better equipped but relied on German-supplied machines plus those that were licence-built in Austria. This Lohner B.II of Fliegerkompanie 6 is at Igalo in mid 1915. (Stach)

Right: The Albatros B.I, here as licence-built examples by Phönix, was a leading type in the first half of the war. The Company had received its first contract for the type in August 1914 and the first of these reconnaissance machines were with front-line units by March 1915. (*FlyPast* Collection)

Below: By 1915 the war had broadened its geographical coverage to include the Mediterranean and Africa. With the Allied campaign in the eastern Mediterranean and Dardanelles came the requirement for air involvement, though this was never on a large scale. Here a Farman F.27 of 3 Wing RNAS is being prepared at Mudros (on the island of Limnos) in 1915. (IWM Q69448)

45

Left: **Nieuport 10 at Imbros 1915.** (Ken Wixey Collection)

Right: **Voisin Type 5 with No 2 Wing, RNAS at Imbros 1915.** (Ken Wixey Collection)

CHAPTER TWO

1916

The conflict entered a new dimension in 1916 with battles on a scale previously undreamed of. Millions of men struggled over a wide front of operation. The year was dominated by two names: Verdun and the Somme. For land and air forces the war became total and uncompromising.

January 1916 saw the RFC on the Western Front go through a comprehensive re-organization with the creation of three air brigades, each comprising a Corps Wing (for artillery co-operation and tactical reconnaissance) and an Army Wing (for strategic reconnaissance, bombing and air fighting). The structure at 30 January was: I Brigade (Aire) with 1 (Corps) Wing and 10 (Army) Wing; II Brigade (Beauval) with 3 (Corps) Wing and 12 (Army) Wing; III Brigade (Oxelaere) with 2 (Corps) Wing and 11 (Army) Wing. No. 4 Brigade was formed at Les Alençons in April.

The January re-organization of the RFC was taking place at a period when the Germans continued to enjoy air superiority. On 14 January the RFC headquarters stated: 'Until the RFC are in a possession of a machine as good as or better than the German Fokker it seems that a change of tactics employed becomes necessary . . . it must be laid down as a hard and fast rule that a machine proceeding on reconnaissance must be escorted by at least three other fighting machines.'

Cecil Lewis was flying reconnaissance sorties with 9 Squadron:

The anti-aircraft bursts had drawn the attention of a roving Fokker to our existence and no sooner were we back on course getting our last two photographs when my Sergeant, now stiffened like a pointer in his set, yelled 'Fokker!' and I turned my head to see the fine slim line of the Hun monoplane rapidly coming up from behind. I managed to get the last photograph just before he opened fire and then heard, as if muffled and far away, the sound of a machine gun. He was firing at us. A second later the

Sergeant's gun was clattering and spewing 'empties', a hole appeared in the windscreen just to the right of my head . . . I had to cut the throttle and put the BE2c into a steep left-hand dive which the Fokker did not follow.

Two new aircraft types joined the RFC in France during January, 20 Squadron arriving with the Royal Aircraft Factory FE2b fighter and 21 Squadron with the RE7. The FE2b (known as the Fee) maintained the pusher design with an observer/gunner in the extreme nose of the aircraft – an exposed but effective position. But despite their manoeuvrability they were soon outclassed in daylight reconnaissance and bombing operations during the Somme offensive, and by 1917 the type's main employment was as a night bomber. The RE7 two-seat reconnaissance-bomber was never a major success and only two units operated the type on the Western Front. The first success for the FE2bs of 20 Squadron came on 7 February while on escort duty to a formation of BE2cs, when they shot down a Fokker.

The Germans continued to refine their fighter organization, and although it was still on a very small scale it pointed the way forward. Typical of this was the creation on 11 January of a dedicated monoplane fighter unit, Eindecker-Kommando-Vaux, with its five Fokker E.IIIs based at Château Vaux, commanded by Oblt. Berthold and under the direct orders of HQ IInd Army. Although there had in the past been local combinations – the Kampfeinsitzer-Kommando (KEK) units – these had been almost informal creations with aircraft still belonging to their original FA. The difference now was that a dedicated fighter unit was created that could train and work together and be moved to areas of the front where it would have the greatest impact. Further such units were created in the early part of 1916 within other German Army areas and also for specialist roles such as

point defence of vital industrial areas, such as Kampfeinsitzer-Kommando-Habsheim near Mülhausen to defend against bomber attacks.

The first major German offensive of 1916 was launched in late February against the French around Verdun. The build-up for this attack had commenced the previous year and air units were moved in from other sectors in order to acquire air superiority. Included in the build-up were reinforced Kaghols I and II to act as strategic bombers and reconnaissance, along with four airships. There were 21 E-types (Fokker and Pfalz variants) and these were soon grouped into three specialist KEK fighter groups.

The ever-important reconnaissance task was of critical value:

The preparation of a photographic map of the region to be attacked was undertaken by a special unit, assisted by the work of four squadrons which had hitherto been confined to the Verdun Front. At the beginning of operations three fighter squadrons were provided to carry out attacks on enemy camps and dumps behind the lines. [P. Neumann, *The German Air Force in the Great War*]

Poor weather in the first few days of the offensive limited the air effort, but before long the air battles over and around Verdun became some of the most fierce of the war to date. A great deal of bombing effort was targeted against the rail communications bringing supplies and reinforcements to the French.

French Response

In the face of the increased German air effort the French too began to concentrate squadrons around Verdun; Cdt. Tricornot de Rose of MS12 was given authority to collect together the best aircraft (Moranes and Nieuports) and pilots in order to achieve air superiority. By 13 March he had a group of 15 pilots gathered at Bar-le-Duc, the first true fighter unit in French service. This organization also applied a new tactical concept: patrols of four or five aircraft were constantly in the air in order to keep the pressure on the opposition. This, and the aggressive nature of the French pilots in their individualistic style, soon wrested control of the air from the Germans. This situation was aided by the fact that with the opening of the British Somme offensive a good proportion of the German air strength was moved to help counter the new threat.

Many of the French aces made their initial reputations during the fierce fighting around Verdun; one such was Jean Navarre who became known as the 'Eagle of Verdun'. He flew with N67 and had his Nieuport 11 painted red all over so that both friends and enemies would know him. To boost the morale of the hard-pressed infantry he would put on flying shows above the lines. His first victory had been on 1 April 1915 in a Morane Parasol of MS12 when his observer, Lt. Robert, had used a Winchester rifle to down an Aviatik reconnaissance aircraft. He claimed his first double victory on 25 February 1916 when he shot down two Fokker E.IIIs but as there was no confirmation it was not until the following day, when he repeated the feat, that he was given due credit. His score had soon increased to twelve but then he was seriously wounded and taken off operational flying. However, by that time other names had begun to emerge and his loss was not the serious blow to morale that it might otherwise have been.

Another unit that saw action here was Escadrille N124 – Escadrille Américaine as it was known, or Escadrille Lafayette from December – manned by American volunteer pilots. The unit had formed on 18 April 1916 and its initial operational fighter complement was of Nieuport 11s.

The DH2 fighters had at last joined the battle over France and in May the GOC (General Officer Commanding) of the 4th Army, Sir Henry Rawlinson, was able to say that 'the de Havilland machine has unquestionably proved itself superior to the Fokker in speed, manoeuvrability, climbing and general fighting efficiency.' Losses were heavy on both sides – as indeed they were on the ground as French determination to hold on to Verdun took on the nature of a crusade. More aircraft were sucked into the combat as each side endeavoured to acquire dominance.

The combining of single-seat Fokker fighters had proved a success elsewhere and so Oswald Boelcke was given the task of forming Sivry Kommando (by 27 June this had become Fokkerstaffel Sivry under the command of Lt. von Hartmann, Boelcke having been grounded following the death of Immelmann). June had been fairly quiet for air combats but on this day the RFC recorded 'a marked increase in the activity of hostile aircraft. Three reconnaissances in force penetrated our lines. On each occasion they were attacked and their formation broken up.' Immelmann had shot down an FE2b in the late afternoon; he took off again that evening and fought with a formation of FE2bs of 25 Squadron, two of whose aircraft were shot down – one perhaps falling to the German ace before he in turn was shot down.

The Fokker was prone to problems with gun synchronization and stoppages, the latter being very difficult to clear in the air because of their position. As historian Alex Imrie points out: 'it gained fame on both sides of the lines because of the results obtained by a relatively small number of pilots and this gave a false impression of its effectiveness to the German High Command.' Most of the pilots knew that what was really needed was a single-seat biplane fighter as this would give far greater manoeuvrability. This became even more apparent after the introduction of the Fokker EIV and Pfalz EIV as they had even poorer overall performance, especially in the vital area of manoeuvrability.

At Verdun, new tactics were being employed by both sides in an effort to gain the upper hand. The Germans had introduced combat groups in September 1915 – and the French had replied with combat pursuit groups in October. By March 1916 the heavy concentration of bombers was being used for defensive patrols; in the face of desperate need the promising French bomber offensive had stalled and was never to recover from this change of air power emphasis. The bomber force went into decline for the rest of the year, partly through the increased stress on the development and production of effective fighters but also through concern at the growing casualty rate on daylight bombing missions. By October this latter factor, re-emphasized on 12 October when five aircraft were lost during an attack on the Mauser factory at Obendorf, had led to the adoption of night bombing. Despite this, calls were still being made for a bomber force of 1,000 aircraft 'as soon as possible'.

Of the bomber designs submitted during the year only those from Breguet showed any promise – especially the Breguet 14. This day bomber was to prove an excellent aircraft but production did not really get under way until early 1917; for the bombing missions of 1916 the squadrons still relied on their Caudrons and Voisins.

Presentation Aircraft

Many of the RFC's aircraft from 1915 onwards were paid for by individuals and well-wishers throughout the Commonwealth. Each aircraft type had a notional price and if they donated this sum of money the aircraft was put into service on behalf of that group, usually with an appropriate inscription.

One of the most active fund-raising organizations was the Australian and Malaysian Battleplane Fund. On 21 May, RE8 C2982 was the first of 94 aircraft to be presented by them; the sponsorship for this aircraft had included £1,300 provided by Eu Tong Sen of Perak and so was named *Eu Tong Sen* in recognition. Donating money to provide such war material was an important aspect of the overall war effort, not really because of the material results but rather for the morale effect of making the donors feel that they were taking an active part in the war effort. This particular fund was organized by C. Alma Baker with an intense campaign of newspaper articles, presentations and pamphlets. A typical plea was:

> Without hesitation or apology, I ask all Australians, to subscribe what they can afford to help to send more of these mighty air engines to our boys, be that help a shilling, a pound, one hundred pounds, a battleplane costing £2,700 or a whole squadron of 16 battleplanes. Can any money you can spare be given to an object of greater value and import than helping to win the war?

While there were some exceptional gifts – like that of the Sultan of Johore who donated a squadron of 16 aircraft – most came from the combined efforts of smaller donations; typical of these was Australia No. 15, a DH5 that cost £2,700 and was inscribed 'NSW No 14, the Women's Battleplane'. Its presentation details read: 'Presented April 12, 1917 by the women of New South Wales and others of which Mrs J S Dunlop subscribed £200, Girls of the National Service Guild, Lismore £117, Mr Justice Hesdon, Sydney

£100, Armidale Battleplane Fund £150, Tweed Battleplane Fund £140'.

Defence of England

The strategic campaign being waged against England by the primarily naval German airships continued, the first attack in 1916 occurring on 31 January when nine of these craft attacked the Midlands (although the planned target was Liverpool).

On 10 February it was announced that responsibility for Home Defence would be transferred to the War Office from the Admiralty, with 'the Navy to undertake to deal with all hostile aircraft attempting to reach this country, while the Army undertake to deal with all such aircraft which reach these shores.' One of the first changes was the amalgamation of ten dispersed fighter flights around London to form 39 Squadron under the command of Maj. T.C.R. Higgins – this was the first of what was to be a number of specialist Home Defence squadrons but the one that was destined to have the most success and to earn the epithet 'Zeppelin Killers'.

The new squadron was equipped with the BE2c and although this type was now being regarded as 'Fokker fodder' on the Western Front, its inherent stability was to make it a good night-fighting platform despite its limited performance. By mid 1916 five such Home Defence squadrons had been formed to cover the main airship target areas and their approach routes, while the RNAS units in their coastal locations continued to provide aircraft for similar duties.

The German airships also flew strategic and tactical raids on targets in France. Typical of these was that of 22 February to Nancy by four airships – of which only one bombed the target area and two were shot down. The growing numbers and effectiveness of fighter aircraft on the Western Front were making it almost impossible for such missions to be flown without unacceptable losses.

However, the greatest promise for the strategic campaign still lay in the offensive against London. April was a very active month, with airship raids mounted on seven nights, four of those being in the first week of the month and with London as the target on six occasions. Despite the fact that more defensive sorties were being flown and more sightings were made, no significant combats occurred and it still seemed that the attackers were having it all their own

way. It was the same story throughout the summer with more raids and more ineffective sorties by the defenders – while the British public and politicians grew increasingly infuriated.

Despite the lack of success, the effort was recognized. A letter to the GOC RFC on 15 April said: 'The Field Marshal C-in-C Home Forces desires to express to you, and through you to the officers and men serving under your command, his appreciation of the excellent organization and skilful and daring action of the RFC allocated to the aerial defence of London.'

The frustration was at last to be relieved in September. One of the defenders scrambled that night was 2nd Lt. William Leefe Robinson in 39 Squadron BE2c '3092 from Sutton's Farm. In the early hours of 3 September he caught up with one of the raiders; after determined attacks using most of his ammunition he reported: 'I had hardly finished this drum when I saw the part fired at glow. In a very few seconds the whole of the rear part was blazing . . . I quickly got out of the way of the falling Zeppelin.' The blazing wreck of the S.L.11 fell at Cuffley. The combat had been witnessed by thousands of cheering Londoners and he was very much the hero of the hour; among the rewards he received was that of a Victoria Cross. The question now was whether this success could be repeated.

The Naval Intelligence Division had now cracked the German airship codes and was able to give more warning of such raids. This was without doubt a significant factor in the improved performance of the defenders. The German Airship Service was determined to prove that it still held the upper hand and planned a major attack on London on 23/24 September. Four of the new 'Super Zeppelins' – the first of these new R-class airships, L-30, having entered service in February – were included in the twelve-strong raiding force. As L-33 approached London it was targeted by anti-aircraft fire and a shell exploded inside the airship, rupturing a gas cell and causing the airship to lose height rapidly. At this point it was attacked by 2nd Lt. Alfred de Bathe Brandon, of 39 Squadron, who caused further damage, and it crashed at Mersea Island. Meanwhile, Brandon saw another airship held by a searchlight beam and headed towards it. Before he could reach his target he saw it fall in flames – another 39 Squadron pilot, Lt. Fred Sowrey, had put three drums of ammunition into the L-32 and it was soon a mass of flames.

The airships returned three more times in 1916 and on two of these attacks lost three more of their number. L-31 fell to 2nd Lt. Wulfstan Tempest (39 Squadron) on 1/2 October, L-34 to 2nd Lt. Pyott (36 Squadron) on 27/28 October and L-21 to two RNAS pilots the same night. The defenders were jubilant and it was considered – prematurely, it turned out – that the airship threat was over.

Naval War

Another aspect of the naval war that the Germans had been looking at for some time was that of the torpedo-carrying aircraft, and on 9 November they finally scored a success:

> At 2 p.m. three torpedo-carrying machines and their fighting escort started. Their orders were 'attack cargo ships off the mouth of the Thames' . . . 3.45 p.m. . . . a few minutes later a merchant ship is sighted, then another, then a third, and finally a whole convoy emerges from the fog. The formation is within range of the hindmost steamer. Three torpedoes drop in quick succession . . . suddenly, one, and a few seconds later, another column of water leaps up at the side of the ship . . . she heels slowly over on to her side and, three minutes later, she disappears.

Problems of Aircraft Supply

May 1916 brought an attempt by the British to solve the inter-service wrangling over aircraft supply through the creation of an Air Board under Lord Curzon: 'The Board shall be free to discuss matters of general policy in relation to the air and, in particular, combined operations of the Naval and Military Air Services, and to make recommendations to the Admiralty and War Office thereon.' It was a good idea but as no executive powers were attached to the Board its work was ineffective and the inter-service problems continued – the Admiralty being particularly obstructive.

The situation in Germany was in some respects worse, especially with regard to the antipathy between the Prussian and Bavarian war ministries, with their associated interests in the units and industries belonging to each state. It was seen as reasonable that Bavarian air units should use Bavarian products – such as the Pfalz – and there was continued wrangling over costs.

By the early spring the RFC had entered another phase of expansion, with more squadrons and an increase in the number of fighter types. April* also brought the Sopwith 1½ Strutter to the Western Front. The additional fighter squadrons and the improved types allowed the RFC to adopt more aggressive tactics and actively go hunting for their enemy. By late April the Fokker 'problem' had been removed and Allied air power was in control.

By July the RFC had 27 operational squadrons in France and although many of these still operated outdated equipment there were a growing number of units with better aircraft such as the DH.2, FE2b and Nieuport. That month the British and French launched what was one of the greatest offensives of the war, and one that has entered history as a great tragedy: the Battle of the Somme. The offensive opened on 1 July as 44 divisions went into the attack on a 15 mile (25km) front. For the RFC the preparatory work had commenced in late June with extensive reconnaissance plus a detailed campaign against German rail links. On 25 June the squadrons carried out widespread attacks on German kite balloons along the entire front and in 15 such attacks claimed five destroyed, four of these falling to Le Prieur rockets. Three more balloons were claimed the next day.

It is important to appreciate the role played by the kite balloons of both sides, and the RFC communiqué for the period 12 to 19 July paid tribute to these units: 'During the operations on the IIIrd and IVth Army fronts, kite balloons have carried out a great deal of useful work, extracts from reports for the period June 26 to July 4 show 239 hostile batteries and 85 other targets located, 41 and 66 respectively being successfully engaged.'

Although the German reconnaissance aircraft were able to provide basic coverage of the British build-up they were aggressively attacked by British and French fighters – the German Air Service was also outnumbered 3:1 on this sector and when the offensive was launched they were quickly overwhelmed, giving the Allies virtual control of the skies. As soon as the offensive had been launched, contact patrols became an important duty, as reflected in an RFC communiqué of 1 July: 'Contact patrols worked continuously on the front of the IIIrd and IVth Armies throughout the day, furnishing most useful information, especially on the front of IIIrd Army where ground communications broke down from 1030 onwards. The

information furnished to Corps HQ by these machines proved to be very accurate.' On 3 July they reported: 'The Commander in Chief directs that all ranks of the RFC should be informed of his high appreciation of the services rendered by them during the last few days. The work done by the RFC has been of material assistance to the Army and has contributed in no small degree to the success of the operations.'

The attacks on German rail communications remained of prime importance; one such mission flown on 1 July was to the St Quentin area by, among others, BE2c aircraft of 12 Squadron and 13 Squadron, each losing two aircraft on this attack. The RFC reported:

> Bombing of the railways north and east of Cambrai, north-east and south-east of Busigny and east of St Quentin was carried out by 12 BEs of 1st Brigade and eight each of 2nd and 3rd Brigades. A train was hit in the middle just south of Aubigny and was set on fire by 2nd Lt Gordon Kidd. 2nd Lt Ellis, seeing the train on fire, came down low and dropped more bombs on it, hitting the rear coaches.

Unusually, the RFC was later able to confirm the effect of the raid through interrogation of German prisoners, one of whom stated:

> About 3.30pm the 1st Battalion of the 71st Reserve Regiment and 11th Reserve Jaeger Battalion were at St Quentin station ready to entrain, arms were piled and the regimental transport was being loaded on to the train. At this moment English aeroplanes appeared overhead and threw bombs. One bomb fell on a shed which was full of ammunition and caused a big explosion. There were 200 wagons of ammunition in the station at the time; 60 of them caught fire and exploded. The train allotted to the transport of the troops and all the equipment which they had placed on the platform were destroyed by fire. The men were panic stricken and fled in every direction.

By mid July the Somme offensive had patently failed to achieve its prime objectives, although the German offensive at Verdun had been halted in response to the new threat in the north. The RFC was by now dominating the battlefield over the Somme and was able to carry out its sorties with little interference. The second half of the summer, as the Somme battles continued, changed the situation once more. A wide range of fighter types was now in oper-

ation with the German Air Service and regular reports were written regarding suitability and requested modifications. One such, dated July 1916, referred to the Halberstadt D.II: 'this aircraft has flown with great success at the Front, and pilots have expressed a high opinion of it in respect of climb performance and manoeuvrability . . . but in all cases a second machine-gun is . . . an urgent requirement.'

When the Somme offensive opened there were two main single-seat fighter formations within IInd Army – KEK Nord at Bertincourt and KEK Süd at Château Vaux – but whereas a few months earlier they had been a dominant force they were now outnumbered and outclassed. But perhaps the most significant move by the Germans during August was the creation of Jagdstaffel (or Jastas): specialist fighter squadrons that were the brainchild of Oswald Boelcke. The first of these, Royal Prussian Jagdstaffel 2 (Boelcke), was formed on 10 August and others followed the same month. These new Jastas were gradually re-equipped with effective aircraft such as the Albatros D.I and D.II, but more important was the change of tactic with the aggressive employment of massed fighters, 'as purely offensive units, they were formed to carry out persistent attacks on enemy aeroplanes and captive balloons and were intended to make it possible at any time to counterbalance the constantly increasing numerical superiority of the enemy at least temporarily, and on any sector of the Front.' [Imrie, *German Fighter Units 1914–1917*]

The first RFC report confirming combat with the new Albatros took place on 31 August, and the new approach was graphically demonstrated on the first Jasta operation by JG2 on 17 September when, led by Boelcke, they encountered a bombing mission by BE2cs of 12 Squadron escorted by FE2bs of 11 Squadron. They promptly shot down four of the escorts as well as two of the bombers. Among the victorious German pilots was Manfred von Richthofen, who claimed the first of what was to be a total of 80 victories for the man destined to be known to history as the 'Red Baron'.

Also in August, Feldmarschall Paul von Hindenburg was appointed as Chief of the General Staff. One of his first directives was to terminate the Verdun offensive and concentrate effort on the Somme battle, and this included a re-allocation of air resources. The net result of the various changes was a rapid loss of Allied air superiority and an ever-increasing number of casualties in the face of fierce German opposition. Despite this, the RFC maintained its offensive and between July and November dropped 18,000 bombs on a variety of targets – railways remaining high on the list. Typical was 15 September when 3 Brigade flew a number of raids:

at Bapaume station, 38 bombs were dropped from heights of 200–800 feet by 12 Squadron with an escort of 11 Squadron. One train, several trucks and the station buildings were repeatedly hit and the rail line badly damaged . . . The bombers came in very low to take good aim and were well protected by the escort; four German machines were brought down and seen to crash . . . two others were driven down out of control.

This raid coincided with the opening of the Battle of Flers-Courcelette – in effect the third phase of the Somme offensive – and was part of the RFC's greatest effort of the war to date.

The increasing losses to the ever-more effective German fighters brought the development of new tactics such as that employed on 25 September:

First Brigade bombing raid on Libercourt – the following scheme to intercept traffic on the Douai–Lille main line was carried out. The railway station at Libercourt was to be bombed and an attempt made to attack trains going south, in the hope that they might be carrying troops or ammunition towards the Somme battlefield. Patrols were first sent to attack the aerodromes at Tourmignies, Phalempin and Provin to prevent German aeroplanes from coming up to interfere.

The FE2bs of 25 Squadron and FE8s of 40 Squadron 'dropped phosphorus bombs at intervals to keep the aerodromes enveloped in smoke, and, from time to time, a 20lb bomb to show that they were still there.'

James McCudden was one of the RFC's leading fighter pilots and a typical air combat of his was recorded as follows. His unit faced two Albatros fighters, but three more joined

what was rapidly developing into a general free-for-all. The fifth remained above, awaiting a suitable moment to enter the fray. Noakes became involved with one opponent for several minutes, the two aircraft circling one another until he managed to turn inside it and fire off two drums while closing to 100 feet. Ball had a lucky escape, being attacked from the rear at very close range as he was changing ammunition drums; he too, had reason to bless the DH2's manoeuvrability, half rolling and getting on the enemy's tail as it

overshot and firing a few bursts from 100 feet. McCudden was also fortunate and by some lucky chance escaped being hit in any vital place by a burst from the rear at only 30 feet. The fight went on for 25 minutes; then as suddenly as they had appeared, the enemy broke off, diving away east.

No. 40 Squadron had been formed at Gosport in February 1916 as the first FE8 unit. It moved to France in August; unfortunately, the type was obsolete by the time it reached the front.

The German bomber force was also still active; Hellmuth Franck served with Kaghol 4 and recalled 'carrying out night bombing missions with the Rumpler C.1 we took-off with six 12.5kg bombs. Once over the target the observer or aerial gunner would pull them out of their case and drop them overboard. One of my first night bombing missions with the Rumpler was a big success. The observer and I had both lost our bearings and finally I called to him to "just get rid of the things anywhere and let's head for home". He dumped the bombs overboard. Suddenly below us there was a great display of fireworks that lasted for hours. We had chanced to ditch our bombs onto a munitions dump!' [Hellmuth Franck, *Cross & Cockade International*, Vol. 19/3]

Meanwhile, the French had also extended the concept of specialist fighter units and created the Groupe de Combat de la Somme by combining the Nieuport 11 equipped N3, N26, N73 and N103 squadrons into this new unit. For a short period it acquired three additional squadrons and became Groupe de Combat 12 – (GC 12 or 'Groupe des Cignones') after the stork motif of its best-known squadron, N3. The effectiveness of this unit was soon proved and in the autumn GC 13 was formed; this and the introduction of the Nieuport 17 gave the Allies the edge in air combat and the German Air Service that suffered heavily. This excellent fighter entered service in May 1916 and was soon to make its mark in the continuing struggle for air superiority. By late summer it had been joined by another of the magnificent French fighters of this period – the Spad VII.

The air battles of Verdun and the Somme had great significance and from that point on there was a definite change in the style of air warfare: 'this battle was wonderful training in everything appertaining to flying, and influenced the entire development of our Air Force in both organisation and design, as well as the methods of training personnel, up to the very end of the war.' [P. Neumann, *The German Air Force in the Great War*]

The two battles had also emphasized the importance of air action, or even air presence, on the morale of the troops in the trenches. A common saying among the German infantry was: 'Has anybody here seen a German [aeroplane]?' (Similar comments were made by British infantry during the 1940 Dunkirk evacuation and emotions ran so high that RAF personnel were physically attacked.) To hear of the exploits of the 'Knights of the Air' not only improved morale with civilians on the Home Fronts but also with the troops in the trenches.

When the German situation improved, 1st Army HQ was quick to report: 'We have received reports from various places on the front to the effect that our aeroplanes are now meeting with more success, and that the infantry are gradually recovering their faith in our air force.'

In his memoirs Gen. Ludendorff paid particular attention to the Somme battles:

On the Somme the enemy had powerful artillery, assisted by excellent aeroplane observation and fed with enormous supplies of ammunition, this kept down our own fire and destroyed our artillery; therefore, the most pressing demands of our offensive were for an increase in artillery, ammunition, aircraft and balloons. Artillery and aircraft were to co-operate more closely. The airmen would have to develop a liking for artillery-ranging work. A battle high up in the air, with a chance of high honours and a mention in Army Orders, was decidedly more exciting and wonderful than ranging for the artillery.

This latter point was one that the French Command cold also make about the attitudes of some of their flyers.

Ludendorff continued:

As early as the Battle of the Somme the enemy aircraft, descending very low, played havoc with our infantry by machine-gun fire, not so much causing heavy casualties as by making troops feel that they had been discovered in places which heretofore they had thought afforded safe cover.

The appearance of the Albatros fighter with its superior performance gave the German fighter units a technical advantage but the French managed to maintain a morale superiority, aided by the astute PR surrounding units such as the famous N3 'Storks' and its bevy of aces. The new German fighter was noted by the RFC on 31 August: '24 Squadron encountered three hostile machines of a new type, extremely fast and climbing quickly. They were bi-planes with stream-lined propeller boss, apparently single-seaters, but firing both in front and over the tail . . . kept above the DH's, diving, firing and climbing again.' The three aircraft were from Jagdstaffel 1 and the DH2s were completely outclassed – it was a pointer of things to come and the loss of the Allied air superiority that had been so hard to win back after the earlier 'Fokker Scourge'.

The DH2s and Nieuports had wrested air superiority from the Fokkers and the Germans had replied with new types such as the Albatros and the creation of highly effective fighter groupings. The more powerful engine of the Albatros DII allowed it to perform well even with two Spandau guns, and this added fire-power was a critical factor in the battle for the skies over Europe. By autumn the Germans had regained their air superiority; the new fighters, such as the Albatros DII, and high morale among the experienced fighter units had forged an effective fighter force that cut swathes through the RFC and French units. Losses on some days were often devastating. Typical of this was 9 November when German fighters attacked an escorted bomber force heading for Vraucourt – nine aircraft were shot down, including four DH2s of 29 Squadron.

The Somme offensive officially ended on 18 November. The RFC suffered 363 aircraft losses and 499 aircrew killed, wounded or missing; German losses were 359. As the Somme battles came to an end, another new type of aircraft entered service with the RFC, with the RE-8 equipped 52 Squadron arriving at Bertangles. A month later the first Sopwith Pup unit, 54 Squadron, moved into the same airfield – so the prospects for 1917 looked somewhat brighter.

The Somme taught many lessons; regarding air power the RFC became convinced that 'more and more it came to be realised that air fighting must govern the future expansion of the Flying Corps' while for ground commanders it was stated that 'aeroplane observation now appears to be an essential preliminary to a successful attack.' These were views held by most of the other air leaders. Field Marshal Haig, a supporter of the role of air power, promptly requested 20 additional squadrons.

Eastern Front

Operations on the Eastern Front remained on a much smaller scale than those in the West, albeit important in their own right and with all the same roles and requirements.

The Russian air arms were slow to expand, with less than 400 aircraft on strength in June 1916. Air units were attached to each of the operational armies, although only at the rate of one fighter squadron per Army until August when a large fighter force was attached to 11th Army. Meanwhile, the Ilya Muromets continued their bombing campaign; despite the increasing threat from fighters, the bomber proved its strength on a number of occasions taking numerous hits and returning home safely.

German strategic planning aimed for a combined air and submarine assault on Britain in the first half of 1917. The main objective was 'the intimidation of the British nation and the crippling of the will to fight, thus preparing the ground for peace.' While unrestricted submarine warfare was to be the main weapon, a bomber offensive against London was considered to be an essential element of the strategy. It was appreciated that to be effective the air arm had to be re-organized; an order dated 8 October 1916 stated:

The increasing importance of the air war requires that all air fighting and defensive forces of the Army, in the field and in the hinterland, be united in one agency. The centralized improvement, preparation and employment of this means of warfare will be assigned to a commanding General of the Air Forces who will be directly subordinate to the Chief of the General Staff.

As part of the re-organization associated with the new strategy an Army Order of 25 November established the Air Force as a separate military branch under the Kommandierender General der Luftstreitkräfte (Commander-General of the Air Force), the first appointee being Gen. Ernst von Hoeppner. He stated that:

Since an airship raid on London has become impossible, the Air Service is required to carry out a raid with aeroplanes as soon as possible. The undertaking will be carried out in accordance with two entirely separate schemes:
  1. Bomber squadrons equipped with G (large) aeroplanes.
  2. Giant flights equipped with R (giant) aeroplanes.
Scheme 1 will be carried out by Half-Squadron No 1 using Gotha G.IV aeroplanes. The requisite number of 30 aeroplanes will be ready by 1 February 1917. By despatching 18 aeroplanes, each carrying a load of 300kg of bombs, 5,400kg could be dropped on London, the same as would be carried by three airships.

The programme was code-named *Türkencruz* and required a complex infrastructure including new airfields near Ghent. Operations were to commence in 1917. However, it was not only the bomber situation that was considered, as Gen. Ludendorff commented: 'At the moment the most important thing was to increase our chaser squadrons and to provide them with a good fighting machine.' These would be the two themes under development in the early part of 1917.

Italy

The ground war between Italy and Austria intensified throughout the year and air operations were accordingly expanded. Both air forces were still inadequately equipped in terms of numbers and capabilities of aircraft; most Italian machines were copies of French types, particularly Farmans and Nieuports.

The Italian Air Service had very quickly decided that offensive bombing was viable and productive, and much attention was paid to this element, with excellent bomber types being produced by the Caproni works. Typical of such attacks was that of 8 September when 58 Caproni bombers, escorted by Nieuports, attacked rail targets in support of the Battle of the Isonzo.

Other Theatres

Although RFC strength in the Middle East was only two squadrons to cover this large area, they took an active part in countering the attempted Turkish attack on Qatiya in April 1916. The previous month a German unit, Flieger Abteilung 300, had arrived at Beersheba to assist the Turkish offensive, equipped with six Rumpler Cs and two Pfalz single-seaters.

Reconnaissance sorties remained paramount for both sides, the Rumplers soon providing photographic coverage of the British lines and installations. In addition to taking photographs, the RFC mounted bombing missions against camps at Bir El Abd and Bir El Bayud: 'the role of the RFC was to reconnoitre the movements of the enemy's troops, co-operate with the monitors which were shelling his camps, prevent hostile reconnaissance from reaching our lines, bomb the enemy camps and personnel, and watch the rear of his positions for reinforcements.' [AP125 p138]

The requirement was similar when the Turks attacked again in August; by this time the RFC had been re-organized by the creation of Middle East Brigade on 7 June with units in Egypt, Salonica (now Thessaloniki), Mesopotamia and East Africa under command. During the August offensive the German machines also undertook attack missions, for example on 4 August at the Battle of Romans six aircraft made a 'squadron attack' using machine guns and bombs to harass troops from low level.

Aircraft remained an important asset in Mesopotamia and the small RFC and RNAS detachments proved invaluable on a number of occasions. In April they even developed a supply dropping technique to get supplies to Kut al Amara and in two weeks dropped 14 tons of food – the average load for each aircraft being 150 to 200lb (70 to 90kg).

Operations in German East Africa, which an Allied force invaded in May, involved 26 Squadron as the main RFC effort plus an RNAS unit. It was difficult terrain and a hard campaign for both sides. Coastal operations were supported by RNAS seaplanes aboard the *Himalaya* and *Laconia*. Dar-es-Salaam was taken on 3 September and the campaign gradually came to an end.

After the Gallipoli disaster, from which the Allies extricated themselves in December 1915, the major elements in the eastern Mediterranean were at Salonica or with the RNAS at Imbros and its associated detached bases throughout the Aegean, from which locations aircraft continued to attack the Turkish and Bulgarian positions. The most mobile element was that of the combined seaplane squadron, comprising the British carriers *Ben-my-Chree* and *Empress* along with the French carriers *Raven II* and *Anne*. For most of the time they operated singly, detaching to various areas in support of other operations; however, they did combine from time to time, for example when three of them joined forces in August to attack the rail link to Haifa.

Conclusions for 1916

As the year ended, the German fighters still held sway and the Albatros DIII was probably the best aircraft at the front in the winter of 1916/17. It 'had pleasant flying characteristics, was well constructed and took into account the experiences of pilots at the Front.' By December 1916 the reliability problems of the Fokker types had reached an extent whereby an order was issued that they were 'henceforth prohibited from use at the Front, mainly as a result of their increasingly poor workmanship. Those machines which remain on order will be used to equip training schools.'

Despite this, Fokker aircraft remained popular with the pilots, partly due, perhaps, to the reputation that Fokker himself had built as a pilot during his frequent liaison visits to units – he was always keen to listen to the opinions of pilots as to what machines they required. However, the Allies had new types in service, especially the Nieuports and Spads, that would soon swing the battle once more – and more new types were due to enter service the following year.

Most of the belligerents realized by the latter part of this year that the many and varied aeroplanes being supplied to their Air Service should be more strictly controlled and that decisions should be taken to reduce the number of different aircraft types by selecting the best for mass production. This was certainly true of Germany; during 1916 some 8,182 aircraft had been delivered and the plan for 1917 was for at least 1,000 machines a month. However, it was easier to state such a plan that it was to implement it in face of problems with the various manufacturers – and government departments.

To indicate the growing strength of the air elements, the table shows aircraft production for the major belligerents in 1916:

Country	1916 Production
Britain	5,716 aircraft
France	7,549 aircraft
Germany	8,182 aircraft
Italy	1,255 aircraft
Russia	1,769 aircraft

Above: By 1916 the air war had changed. Gone were the days of small numbers and 'aerial chivalry', it was now ferocious and deadly. This desolate scene of unknown date shows two aircraft crash-landed amidst a barren battleground. This was a common site as attempts were made to force enemy aircraft down behind friendly lines while they in turn tried to make it back to their own side. (Ken Delve Collection)

Left: The RE7 was designed as a two-seat reconnaissance/bomber and initial contracts had been issued in 1915. However, it was in January 1916 that the first fully equipped unit, 21 Squadron, deployed to France. The type had serious shortcomings and only two operational squadrons used it in France. (Ken Delve Collection)

Right: Aircrew of 21 Squadron at Boisdinghem. Left to right: 2nd Lt. Russell, 2nd Lt. E. Townsend, Lt. W. Bishop (of later ace fame), 2nd Lt. Scaramanga, 2nd Lt. Digby-Johnson, Lt. Lord George Dundas. The Squadron had re-equipped with the RE7 in mid 1915 but moved to France in early 1916; most of its operational sorties were bombing. (Ken Delve Collection)

Above: **By early 1916 the FB5 'Gunbus' was completely outclassed, causing Trenchard to comment: 'it is essential that these machines be replaced by something better at an early date.'** (Ken Delve Collection)

Below left: **Although ungainly in appearance, the FE2b was reasonably effective when it first appeared operationally in early 1916; however, it was not the great success in the fighter-reconnaissance role that had been hoped.** (Ken Delve Collection)

Below right: **The first FE2bs were delivered to 20 Squadron in December 1915 and the following month the unit moved to France. This two-seat pusher was ordered in large quantities from a variety of contractors and throughout 1916 was one of the most important aircraft on the RFC's operational strength. This particular aircraft, '6338, was a presentation aircraft – Ceylon No 3 – with 20 Squadron.** (Peter Green Collection)

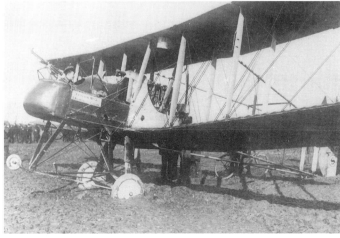

Left: **FE2b A5666 with the 160hp Beardmore engine. This engine gave even more trouble than the other fits – and it must be born in mind that many of the engines in use were not particularly reliable – and caused much adverse comment. The Fees generally proved inadequate as fighters but appeared at a time when there was little else; however, they soon found a new role as bombers as this role grew in importance throughout 1916.** (Harry Holmes)

Right: **The FE2b carried a variety of armament but the commonest arrangement was for two (sometimes three) Lewis guns, the mounts for which can be seen here. The rear mount allowed the observer to fire back over the wing.** (Capt. D.S. Glover)

Left: **The FE2d resulted from an attempt to re-equip the FE2b with a more powerful engine such as the 250hp Rolls-Royce. It was never truly a success but the type entered service on the Western Front and for Home Defence from mid 1916.** (Peter Green Collection)

Right: Powered by a 110hp Gnome Monosoupape, the FE8 was employed as a single-seat fighter on the Western Front from summer 1916 to early 1917 but its speed of 80mph (130kph) and single Lewis gun meant that it was hopelessly outclassed. The type also served with Reserve Squadrons in the UK as here with '6401 with 10 Reserve Squadron at Joyce Green. (Capt. D.S. Glover)

Left: DH2 '7851 with 32 Squadron, which it probably joined in summer 1916.

Below: DH2 '5943 built by the Aircraft Manufacturing Company and fitted with the 100hp Gnome Monosoupape. (*FlyPast* Collection)

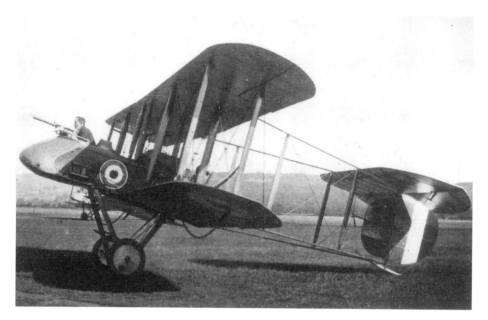

Left: The only front-line unit to use the FB9 was 11 Squadron, which acquired the prototype in January 1916 for operational trials. This was a standard procedure with new aircraft types being used by selected squadrons in action to assess the true potential of the type. The FB9 seemed promising despite a poor gun mounting and the type was put into production; however, by July 1916 the few that had reached operational status were withdrawn. (Peter Green Collection)

Right: Designed as a two-seat fighter-reconnaissance aircraft, the FB14 looked a good design and was ordered into production off the drawing board. In the event, however, only six of these Vickers aircraft were allocated to the RFC (and ten to Home Defence in 1917). A686 is seen at Farnborough in 1916. (Peter Green Collection)

Left: Martinsyde Elephants of 27 Squadron at Fienvillers in 1916. The Squadron had arrived in France in March, having formed with the Martinsyde G.100 at Hounslow Heath the previous November, as a scout Squadron. With a speed of almost 90mph (145kph) and good manoeuvrability, the Martinsydes were effective when they first entered service. (Peter Green Collection)

Right: **The RNAS operated a small number of Breguet pushers with 5 Wing from spring 1916. Despite its fairly high-powered 225hp Sunbeam Mohawk engine, the aircraft could only achieve 86mph (138kph) and a ceiling of 12,140ft (3,700m).** (Peter Green Collection)

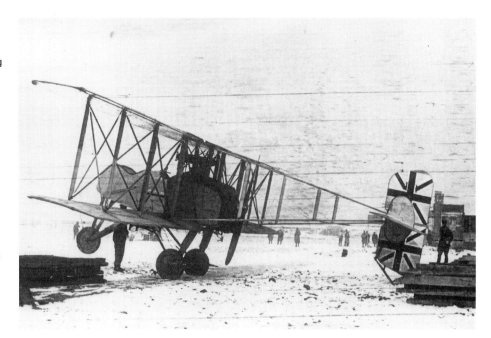

Below: **Good upper view of a 2 Squadron BE2c. This type remained in significant numbers on the Western Front during 1916 and was very vulnerable; losses were high as the performance of the aircraft was now grossly inferior to that of the enemy fighter types.** (Ken Delve Collection)

Above: The success of the BE2c led directly to the creation of the more powerful single-seat BE12, the first contracts for which were issued in late 1915. Entry to service did not come until spring 1916 with the Home Defence units but it was not long before the type was also in use on the Western Front. (Peter Green Collection)

Left: **BE12, probably at Farnborough.** (Harry Holmes)

Below right: **BE12a A4040 crashed behind enemy lines killing the pilot. His body is shown in another photo from this sequence of pictures that were 'liberated' from a Bulgarian trench. Note the twin guns mounted on the upper wing.** (Ken Delve Collection)

Right: Aircraft losses were due not only to enemy action; indeed, most losses were in accidents or, as here, 'natural causes'. These five BE12s of 21 Squadron were wrecked within five days of their delivery to the Squadron at Boisdingem when the hangar was 'destroyed in a freak storm in autumn 1916'. (Ken Delve Collection)

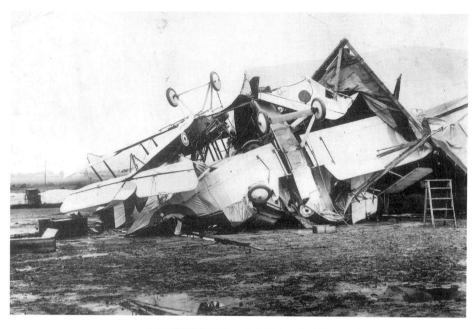

Left: Work on the RE8 general purpose two-seater to replace the BE2c began in late 1915 and the prototype ('7996) first flew in June 1916; the type entered service with 52 Squadron in November. (Harry Holmes)

Below: RE8 A3570 was a Daimler-built example of this widely used and reasonably effective type – some 2,262 RE8s were built. (Ken Delve Collection)

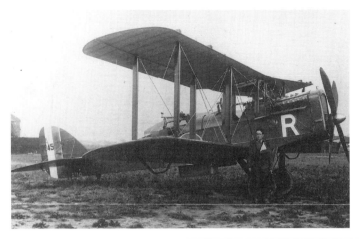

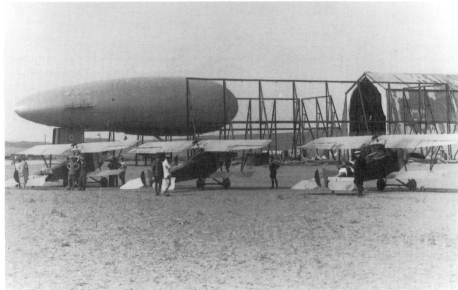

Above left: One of the most prolific – and best – of British designs, the DH4 had a long and distinguished operational record. The type first flew in August 1916 and it looked a winner from the start; indeed, a production order had been issued the previous month! A7845 is seen here with 202 Squadron. (Peter Green Collection)

Above right: Although the Bristol Scout D had made its first appearance in late 1915, it was the following year before they became operational with the RNAS. Some 80 Scouts Ds were ordered by the RNAS, a number of which were handed to the RFC during the summer. (*FlyPast* Collection)

Centre: Nieuport 12 two-seaters at Mudros in 1916, with an SS type airship in the background. (Ken Wixey Collection)

Right: The British continued to use French machines; here a Morane BB biplane in service with 60 Squadron in June 1916, one of four RFC units on the Western Front to operate the type. (Capt. D.S. Glover)

Above: **During 1916 a number of new types were in their design and development stage; such was the Bristol F2A, another machine seen as a replacement for the BE2c. The type first flew in September 1916 and initial deliveries were made before the end of the year. 48 Squadron was the only fully equipped unit but the type led to the F2B – one of the best general-purpose aircraft of the war and one that had a lengthy post-war career.** (*FlyPast* Collection)

Right: **Reconnaissance remained the primary role, with photographic reconnaissance now considered an essential element of any offensive plan. This 2 Squadron shot shows the devastated town of Ypres.** (Ken Delve Collection)

Below: **A photograph dated 30 March 1916 of the Hohenzollern redoubt. Comprehensive photography of the extensive trench systems was a pre-requisite of all the major attacks.** (Ken Delve Collection)

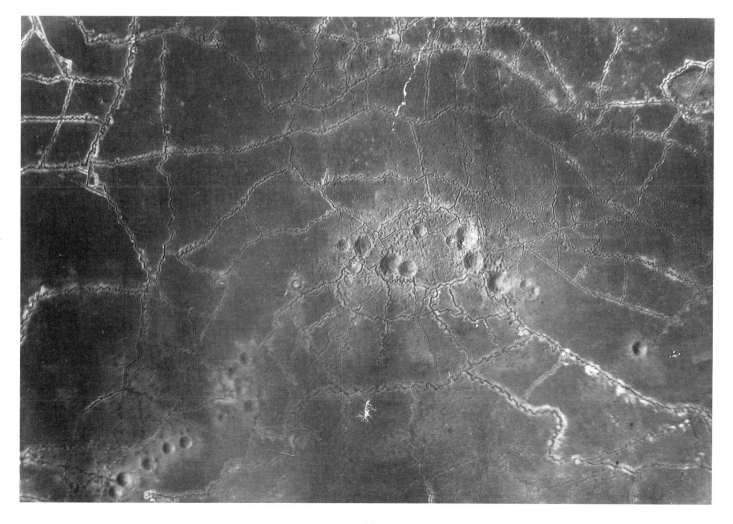

Above right: **2nd Lt. William Leefe Robinson of 39 Squadron, who was awarded the Victoria Cross following his victory over the German airship.** (Ken Delve Collection)

Above left: **A few days later the L33 was also shot down though a combination of anti-aircraft fire and the attentions of another 39 Squadron pilot, 2nd Lt. Alfred de Bathe Brandon. The Zeppelin crashed at Mersea Island.** (Peter Green Collection)

Below left: **Although the BE2c was by mid 1916 outdated and vulnerable on the Western Front, its inherent stability well suited it for the task of Home Defence and when the RFC took over responsibility for this task from the RNAS it was the BE2c that formed the bulk of the defending fighters to counter the night raids by German Zeppelins. The first success came on the night of 2/3 September 1916 when William Leefe Robinson of 39 Squadron shot down the SL.11. Here the pilot poses in the cockpit of his BE2c – the object being held by the airmen is part of his aircraft that he damaged during the combat.** (Ken Delve Collection)

Above left: The same night that L33 fell, 23/24 September, another fell to the guns of 39 Squadron when Lt. Fred Sowrey destroyed the L32. Sowrey is seen here in the cockpit of BE2c '4112. 39 Squadron scored another victory on 1/2 October, when 2nd Lt. Wulfstan Tempest destroyed the L31. L34 was also shot down the same night. (Ken Delve Collection)

Above right: Commander of the L33, Kapitän-Leutnant Alois Bocker (left) held prisoner after the loss of his airship. (Peter Green Collection)

Right: Although this photograph of 39 Squadron dates from early 1917 at Sutton's Farm, it shows the three confirmed Zeppelin destroyers. Left to right, standing: Capt. Stammers, Lt. W.J. Tempest, Lt. W. Leefe Robinson, Lt. Fred Sowrey, Capt. Bowers. Seated: Lt. C.L. Brock, Lt. C. Durston, L. Mallinson. (Ken Delve Collection)

Left: The BE2c was usually flown as a single-seater by the Home Defence units in an effort to improve its performance; it was self-evident therefore that the BE12 would also find its way to the Home Defence units. This Le Prieur equipped BE12a served with 50 Squadron in this role. (Peter Green Collection)

Above left: Capt. Hadoi airborne in a BE12b of 50 Squadron. The Squadron used the type from May 1916 to June 1918, although from 1917 it was supplemented with other types such as the RE8 and Sopwith Pup. (Ken Delve Collection)

Above right: BE12b of 76 Squadron, another of the Home Defence units that operated the type for two years from 1916. The Home Defence organization expanded rapidly from late 1916 although it was equipped with BE2 and BE12 variants, which were soon outclassed. The euphoria over 39 Squadron's string of victories in late 1916 soon gave way to growing frustration. (Ken Delve Collection)

Centre right: The Germans had been using aircraft for strategic bombing from 1915 and by 1916 a range of new types was available such as this Gotha GIII – although only used in small numbers on the Western Front and with no great measure of success. (MAP)

Left: The AEG GIII was likewise only produced in small numbers and was operational by spring 1916. Among other users was Kaghol 1, which employed the type during their involvement on the Macedonian Front. The aircraft was powered by two 220hp Mercedes DIV engines, which gave it a very respectable 98mph (158kph) speed. (Ken Delve Collection)

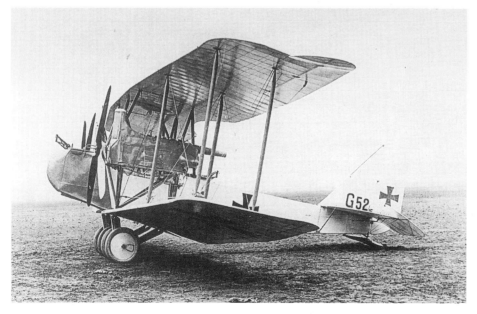

Right: The AEG GIV with the 260hp Mercedes DIVa entered service towards the end of the year and continued in use until mid 1918. This example is a captured aircraft. (Capt. D.S. Glover)

Left: The training organizations of all the belligerents had to expand to meet the requirements of the front-line units; suitable aircraft were often in short supply. The RNAS and RFC made use of Curtiss JN-4 Jennies such as '8820 seen here at Redcar in September 1916 to supplement its training types. (Capt. D.S. Glover)

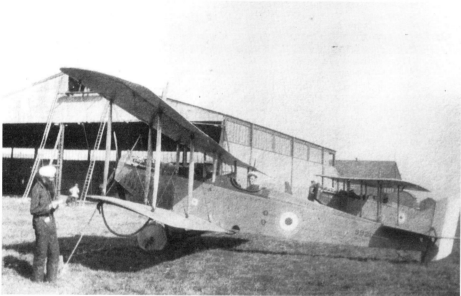

Right: The BE2e was, like other BE2 variants, extensively used for trials and training duties as well as operationally. Its basic flying characteristics, reliability and rugged nature made it a good training machine. This particular example, C7133, is seen with 31 Training Squadron at Wyton in May 1918. (Capt. D.S. Glover)

Above: **A number of captured German aircraft spent time with training and trials units; here an Albatros is at Gosport with one of the most famous of all exponents of flying training, Maj. R.R. Smith-Barry.** (Ken Delve Collection)

Right: **By 1916 French air strength had become impressive, and with types such as the Nieuport and Spad the fighter units had capable equipment. The Nieuport 17, as N2474 here, was powered by a 110hp Le Rhône and had a top speed of 110mph (177kph).** (Peter Green Collection)

Left: **Transfer of aircraft was not all one way, and several types were licence built, Nieuports and Spads, for example, being built in England while the Sopwith 1½ Strutter was built in France as the 1A2.** (Peter Green Collection)

Above: **A variety of Allied aircrew posing in front of a Spad VII. The prototype of this great fighter first flew in April 1916 and it soon entered production. Designed by Louis Béchereau, this was without doubt one of the best fighters of the war.** (Ken Delve Collection)

Below left: **Following on from earlier Nieuports in RNAS service, the Nieuport 11 'Bébé' is here as '3982 of 2 Squadron RNAS – part of 1 Wing at Dunkirk. The Bébé became operational with Escadrille N3 in January 1916 and was an immediate success.** (Peter Green Collection)

Below right: **The Nieuport 11 established a good reputation and the basic Nieuport design characteristics began to appear in a number of aircraft; these are at Luxeuil in May 1916.** (via Icare)

Left: **Nieuport 17, possibly of Escadrille N76. This Nieuport was built in large numbers and equipped many of the French fighter squadrons, as well as a variety of Allied units.** (Jack Bruce)

Right: **The Nieuport squadrons played a vital role in wresting air superiority from the Germans around Verdun and over the French sectors south of the Somme. This Nieuport 17 served with Escadrille N3.** (Jean Devaux)

Below: **The Spad VII with its 150 or 180hp Hispano-Suiza engine had a top speed of 119mph (192kph) and was yet another of the superb French fighter designs that appeared from mid 1916 onwards.** (MAP)

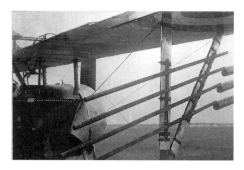

Above: **Le Prieur incendiary rockets fitted to a French Nieuport. They were fired electrically, and one of their main uses was against balloons – and attempts against Zeppelins.** (Ken Wixey Collection)

Right: **Among the French aces to establish a reputation on Nieuports and Spads was Charles Guynemer. Here he poses with a Spad VII in December 1916.** (Dennis Hylands)

Above: **Voisin Type 8/10 (both variants similar) two-seat bomber in used from 1916, it had a speed of only 82mph (132kph) and a ceiling of 14,110ft (4,300m) but by operating at night was reasonably safe.** (Ken Wixey Collection)

Right: **A robust and reliable bomber, the Caudron R4 was somewhat lacking in performance and was eventually replaced by the RXI.** (Ken Wixey)

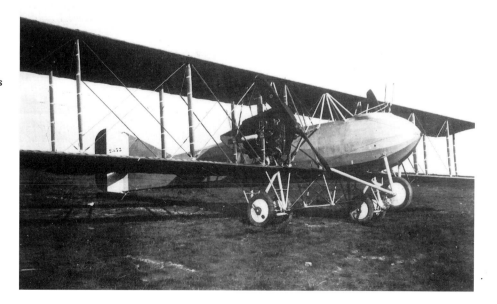

Left: **Spad XIII C.1.** Powered by the geared 220hp Hispano, the Spad XIII was fast, but not as manoeuvrable as the Spad VII. (Jack Bruce/Stuart Leslie collection)

Right: **Nieuport 11 in German hands.** (Jack Bruce/Stuart Leslie collection)

Left: **The Aviatik CI was still in use during 1916 but was outclassed by the latest British and French fighters, leading to increased losses and a reluctance to cross the Allied lines on reconnaissance. This particular example, as can be seen from the rudder markings, is a captured aircraft.** (Capt. D.S. Glover)

Right: The DFW CV was used in large numbers from 1916 to the end of the war in a variety of roles. Note the distinctive 'fish tail'. (MAP)

Below: The LFG Roland CII, of which several hundred were built, entered service in early 1916 as a reconnaissance aircraft but was also used as an 'escort fighter.' (Schmitt)

Right: Albatros CIIIs entered service on the Western Front in the winter of 1916; the type was built in large numbers by a variety of manufacturers. Powered by either a 150hp Benz BzIII or 160hp Mercedes DIII it had a top speed of 87.5mph (141kph). (Heinz Birkholz)

Left: **Staffel 39 Albatros CVI at Artemps in 1916. Although produced in only limited numbers this was an effective reconnaissance type. In essence it was a DIII variant with a 180hp Argus AsIII engine.** (Plickert)

Right: **A direct follow-on from the DII, the Halberstadt DIII performed reasonably well during 1916; it served on into spring 1917 pending delivery of new single-seat scout deliveries but by then its speed of 90mph (145kph) and single Spandau were simply not adequate.** (Ken Delve Collection)

Left: **French soldiers inspect this captured Rumpler CI. By 1916 the type was an important general-purpose aircraft and was well liked by its crews. When eventually outclassed on the Western Front it went on to serve in other theatres.** (Capt. D.S. Glover)

Right: **AEG GIII**. (Ken Wixey Collection)

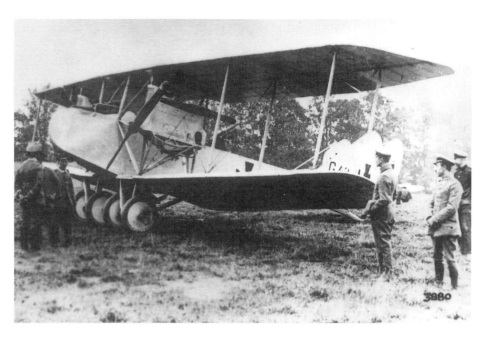

Left: In British markings, this LVG CII was photographed by Capt. D.S. Glover when it was under test with the RFC. The CII had first appeared in late 1915 and by 1916 was in widespread use. (Capt. D.S. Glover)

Below: The Albatros DI was introduced to counter the DH2 and early Nieuports that had proven superior to the Fokker Eindeckers. Along with the DII they became standard equipment for the new fighter units – the Jastas. (Ken Delve Collection)

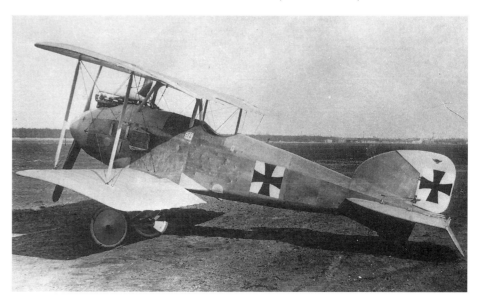

Above left: **Euler C-type under test in mid 1916; note the armament of two parabellum machine guns. This, along with the Spandau, was a very effective aerial weapon and a success for German machine gun technology.** (MAP)

Above right: **Kurt Wintgens was one of the early aces, becoming one of the first members of Jasta 1 when it formed. He was killed in action on 25 September 1916 while engaging a Nieuport.** (Dennis Hylands)

Centre: **Intended for training use, the Euler Dr4 was put forward in 1916 and was one of the only types to have side-by-side seating for the crew.** (MAP)

Below: **The Albatros CVII entered service late in 1916 and by the following February some 350 were in use for reconnaissance and artillery observation.** (MAP)

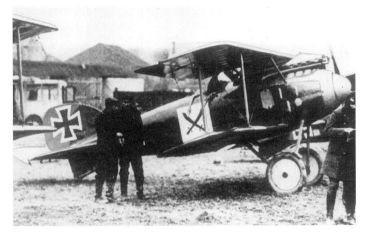

Left: One of the new fighter types to enter service in autumn 1916, the Albatros DII went to the Jastas in their bid to regain air superiority. The aircraft relied on its speed and fire-power of two Spandaus as it was not the most manoeuvrable fighter at the front. (MAP)

Right: The Roland DII first flew in October 1916 and entered service early the following year. It was a development of the DI, itself a single-seat development of the CII. The type was not a great success as it was too heavy on the controls for a fighter, but some 300 of the D1/II/IIa were built. (MAP)

Below: The Eastern Front remained very much a ground war although air operations did grow in importance during 1916; the Russians continued to rely on foreign aircraft, such as this Nieuport 17. (*FlyPast* Collection)

Left: The Jastas were highly successful in regaining air superiority at any point on the front to which they were attached; however, the problem was that there were simply not enough of them to cover all areas. This Albatros DI belonged to Karl Büttner of Jasta 2 in late 1916. (Ken Delve Collection)

Below: The Germans and Austrians continued to dominate the air scene in the East with superior numbers of better aircraft; types that were outclassed on the Western Front were often transferred to the East where they still proved effective. This Oeffag CI is over Galicia. (Kostrba)

Above left: **Lohner BVII of Fliegerkompanie 16 in autumn 1916; up to mid 1915 this had been an aircrew training unit but in May it moved to the Carinthian Front for operations, remaining operational as a 'general purpose' unit until the end of the war.** (Grosz)

Above right: **Single bay version of the AEG CVII; the type was in production in late 1916** (MAP)

Right: **The redoubtable Fokkers played their part on the Isonzo Front, as with this E.I of Fliegerkompanie 4 at Haidenschaft in February 1916.** (Kostrba)

Below: **The major area of conflict between the Italians and Austrians was in the Isonzo area and this became the scene of numerous air battles, although most air effort was applied in direct support of the ground forces. These Maachi-built Nieuport 11s were standard equipment for a number of units.** (IWM Q68869)

Above: The campaigns in the Middle East continued to include air participation, albeit still on a small scale but often with decisive results. This Martinsyde S1 ('4250) is pictured at an unknown airfield in Egypt where it was probably in use for training. However, the 30 Squadron detachment in Mesopotamia had used two of this type with some success and this aircraft may have been destined for the same unit. (Ken Delve Collection)

Above: Following the Dardanelles fiasco, the Allies maintained an air presence on land and with seaplane carriers in the eastern Mediterranean. This Nieuport 12 ('8731) was at Mudros in November 1916. (Ken Delve Collection)

Right: The Australia and Malaya Battle Planes Fund was one of a number of such organisations raising funds to provide 'presentation aircraft'. This particular fund supplied 49 aircraft, although 16 of these came from the Sultan of Johore. (Ken Delve Collection)

ILLUSTRATIONS ON THE COVERS OF APPEAL PAMPHLETS

Battleplanes at Work with Artillery
Preparing for a Bloodless Advance
HELP TO SAVE THESE BOYS' LIVES ! !
A HALF-CROWN OR MORE WILL DO IT
Every additional Battleplane may save thousands of Lives
and Countless Casualties
Lend the Boys a Hand   No subscription too Small
YOUR BATTLEPLANE will be FIGHTING BEFORE THREE MONTHS

What YOUR Subscription to a Battleplane
may help to accomplish for the Empire
The Value of Aircraft in cut-
ting off enemy reinforcements
WHAT COMMAND OF THE AIR
MEANS TO US

CHAPTER THREE

1917

On 1 January the British delivered an example of their brand-new bomber type to the Germans when HP 0/100 '1463 landed in error at a German airfield on its delivery flight from the UK in poor weather. The aircraft was soon under intensive test by the Germans: it was not an auspicious start to 1917.

'In the beginning of the year there was a repetition of the Fokker period. The new German Albatros and Halberstadt fighters, with their twin synchronised machine-guns, exacted a heavy toll amongst both fighter and reconnaissance aeroplanes of the RFC, and the superiority we had on the Somme for the time definitely passed to the enemy.' [AP125 p186]

Haig had, at the end of December 1916, made the impending situation quite clear: 'I desire to point out that the maintenance of mastery of the air, which is essential, entails a constant and liberal supply of the most up-to-date machines, without which even the most skilful pilots cannot succeed.' At this stage only the Sopwith Pup could match the performance of the German fighters and was available only in small numbers. Of the other new types, the RE8 had a poor initial reputation with a series of accidents that led 52 Squadron to re-equip with the out-performed BE2e.

It was not until March that new fighter types began to reach the Western Front to help redress the balance. The Airco DH4 arrived with 55 Squadron and the Bristol F2B with 48 Squadron – both types had a great future but there were growing pains to suffer first. In April they were followed into service by the SE5. The FK8 was another of the new British types to enter service in 1917, arriving at St Omer with 35 Squadron as part of the continued search for an effective two-seat reconnaissance and bomber aircraft.

Allied reconnaissance observed major construction work taking place behind the German lines as a new defensive system (later to be known as the Hindenburg Line)

was created. The German withdrawal to the new positions began on 14 March, the retreat being monitored and harassed by Allied air power. Then, on 9 April, Haig launched his next major offensive – the Battle of Arras, which was to last until 17 May – primarily by the 20 Divisions of Third Army. It was to go down in RFC history as 'Bloody April'. Haig later said:

> a period of very heavy air fighting ensued . . . losses on both sides were severe, but the offensive tactics most gallantly persisted in by our fighting aeroplanes, secured our artillery aircraft from serious interference, and enabled our guns to carry out their work effectively. At the same time, bombarding aircraft caused great damage and loss to enemy by a constant succession of raids directed against his dumps, railways, aerodromes and billets. [AP125 p191]

This official (RAF) account of this period stressed the problems faced by the RFC, observing that

> the German Air Service enjoyed in the Spring of 1917 the zenith of its power. By anticipating the British in the production of new fighters, the Germans sprang the second, and last, surprise on the British Air Forces. Not only were the fighter aeroplanes of superior performance but they also formed the first Circus. This was achieved by the close grouping of No 3, 4, 11 and 33 *Jagdstaffeln* which were attached to the Arras Corps.

In fact, the fighter force available on the Arras Front in April comprised Jastas 3, 4, 11, 12, 27, 28, 30 and 33 but losses were so severe that units were often down to an effective strength of only a handful of aeroplanes and the problems of re-supply of pilots and aircraft made the situation little short of desperate. Nevertheless, the German fighters had established a morale and physical dominance and achieved a victory ratio of four to one. The first formal grouping took place in June under Manfred

von Richthofen. It existed purely to achieve air superiority at any given point on the front, hence its first period of operations was over Flanders. This mobility of 'élite' units was not unique to the Germans as the French, and to a lesser extent the British, also made use of the tactic from time to time.

There was a difference between the English and French fronts:

> The enemy aerial activity was numerically the superior, but in no phase of the battle did it gain tactical advantage over us. Also, aerial battles were not pursued so determinedly as on the English front, as the French, although gallant, were not so keen. Long combats, such as were common on the English front, were the exception on the French. [P. Neumann, *The German Air Force in the Great War*]

It was during parts of this battle that the RFC's squadrons began to undertake ground attack missions in support of the infantry (what would in later conflicts be called 'close air support'). Typical of this was the mission flown on 3 May – the first day of the Battle of the Scarpe – by five Sopwith 1½ Strutters of 43 Squadron when they strafed German infantry massing for a counter-attack. This particular squadron did much to develop this very hazardous role, a role that became increasingly important. The same was true of the German Air Service with the first employment of dedicated close air support units known as 'storm flyers' (Sturmflieger).

Typical of the German references to this work is that for 6 September in association with the evacuation of Péronne: 'from the grey light of dawn until late in the evening our trench-strafing machines were in the air striving to relieve our hard-pressed infantry, and they were on the ground barely long enough to be prepared for the next flight.'

On 7 June the next British attack was launched – the Battle of Messines, an attack that was presaged by the almost simultaneous explosion of 20 huge mines and bombardment by over 2,000 pieces of artillery. As the infantry pressed forward the RFC flew contact patrols, a technique that had by now been almost perfected, as well as extensive counter-battery work; however, at least four squadrons were also given free rein to roam the battlefield in the close air support role.

Bombing missions of a more strategic nature were still taking place, the RNAS, as before, taking a leading part. In February a concerted day and night bombing offensive was launched against docks and airfields around Bruges: 'in a determined effort to make these untenable to the enemy, vigorous and systematic bombing attacks were made.'

The Airco DH4, although originally intended for the two-seat fighter and reconnaissance role when it entered service in early 1917, was in fact destined to establish a solid reputation as a day bomber. As the amount of day bombing increased so the role of the DH4 equipped units became more important. The RFC now had five brigades deployed in France, each comprising two wings of up to six squadrons, plus the GHQ Wing of seven squadrons at Fienvillers.

The Germans maintained their air superiority through the early summer and the RFC suffered a great loss on 7 May with the death of the renowned air ace Albert Ball. Another single-seat fighter joined the ranks in May with the arrival of the DH5, an aircraft with reasonable performance but hampered by a poor field of view for the pilot. This was followed in June by the Sopwith Camel, one of the truly great fighters – although the type had already been with 4 (Naval) Squadron since the end of May.

U-boat War

At the beginning of February 1917 the Germans had resumed their unrestricted U-boat war and this was by April causing major worries with an average of five ships being sunk each day. The air elements of the anti U-boat campaign increased the number of their patrols and the areas that were being covered; in an eighteen-day period from 13 April they flew twenty-eight patrols, which resulted in eight sightings and three attacks.

The bulk of this work was still being performed by the various flying boats operating from, for example, Felixstowe, with patrol lines set up along the U-boat transit areas as well as around specific shipping routes. Although actual sinkings were still not common, a Curtiss H.12 Large America flying boat did sink the UC-36 on 20 May, and the presence of the aircraft restricted the operations of the submarines. The Large America was introduced into the RNAS in the spring of 1917, the first operation taking place on 13 April by aircraft '8661 from Felixstowe. The type was used against airships as well as submarines.

From early May the German Navy began sending 'fighter seaplanes' to try to destroy the patrolling RNAS , aeroplanes, the Brandenburg series of two-seat fighter seaplanes proving particularly effective in this role. In reply the RNAS put greater weight of armament on their flying boats and, in keeping with aggressive Naval tradition, sent aircraft to attack the enemy bases – to which their adversaries replied in kind with attacks on Felixstowe. However, further U-boat kills were made, UC-1 being claimed on 24 July and UB-20 on 29 July. The German fighter seaplanes did take a toll of the new British NS (North Sea) airships that had entered service in April for convoy duty, the first of which, NS1, went to the station at Pulham.

The German Navy also used airships in connection with the extensive minefields that both sides were now employing. The British were laying up to 10,000 mines a month as part of the anti U-boat campaign: 'by buoys dropped from the airship, we were able to mark the boundaries of any minefields that were sighted, and could thereby indicate their position to our mine sweepers. The unceasing airship patrols made it possible for the mine sweepers to carry out their arduous labours unmolested by the enemy.' [P. Neumann, *The German Air Force in the Great War*]

Experience had now shown, however, that Zeppelins were not ideal for long-range reconnaissance over the North Sea so thought was given to developing the now almost redundant torpedo-bombing aircraft for this role as they had an endurance of over 10 hours – in the event this too was to prove only partially successful.

The other important development in naval terms was the desire to have effective aircraft working with the Royal Navy's Grand Fleet, in particular for defensive work against airships and aircraft. Thus various methods were examined by the Grand Fleet Aircraft Committee of putting fighter-type aircraft aboard warships. In due course the light cruiser HMS *Yarmouth* was given a

'flying platform' and in June Flt. Cdr. F. Rutland flew a Sopwith Pup from this precarious position. Further trials followed, and the first operational success came on 21 August when Sub. Lt. B.A. Smart launched in his Pup (his first such take-off) to engage a shadowing Zeppelin. He caught and destroyed the L-23 and after the combat ditched his aircraft and was picked up by HMS *Prince*.

To increase the availability of fighter aircraft with the Fleet, platforms were fitted above gun turrets, trials for this being carried out aboard HMS *Repulse* in early October: 'these two flights having demonstrated the practicability of carrying aeroplanes on the turrets of capital ships without interfering with the sighting of that turret's guns or the fighting efficiency of the ship, it was decided to fit similar platforms for single seaters to all battle cruisers.' By early 1918 some nine ships had been fitted with platforms, each for two Pups, and trials were underway with the use of two-seat aircraft as these were considered better for a range of other roles.

The final element in naval development this year was that of the aircraft carrier. In March it had been decided to restructure the light cruiser HMS *Furious* with a flight deck and a hangar for the operation of ten aircraft; initial flight trials on the new carrier were flown in August by Sq. Cdr. E.H. Dunning in a Pup. The lessons of this and other trials led to modifications and the vessel did not enter service until March 1918. In the meantime the Admiralty planned to construct four other carriers, each with a speed of 25 knots (45kph). Most were conversions from existing ships, and none were ready to enter service in 1917.

America Enters the War

The nature of the war changed markedly on 6 April when America declared war on Germany and her allies, President Woodrow Wilson stating that 'the world must be made safe for democracy.' It would be some time before American forces would be in a position to influence the conflict but the longer-term implications of the announcement were quickly appreciated by others, including Gen. Ludendorff on 25 June: 'The entry of America into the war obliges us to strengthen our aerial forces by 1st March 1918. A minimum of 40 new fighter squadrons must be set up if our forces are to be a match for the combined English-French-American aerial fleet.' This became known as the America Programme.

The American military was in no shape to take part in the war without a great deal of re-organization and re-equipping and the pressure was on to carry this out as quickly as possible. May saw a military mission, led by Maj. Raynal Bolling, tour Britain, France and Italy to see what aircraft being used by the Allies could be adopted for use by the United States Air Service (USAS). They examined a variety of aircraft and manufacturers and spoke to government agencies concerning production details and contracts. Among the many comments made by Bolling in his August report was one that supported strategic bombing:

> There is practically no effective means of preventing night bombing, therefore its possibilities appear to depend almost entirely on the number of suitable aeroplanes which can be provided . . . could night bombing be conducted on a sufficiently great scale and kept up continuously for a sufficient time, there seems good reason to believe that it might determine the whole outcome of military operations.

By August contracts had been issued for 5,000 aircraft and 8,500 engines from the French aviation industry – while at the same time making licence agreements with other manufacturers, the most significant of which was for the British DH.4 intended for long-range reconnaissance and day bombing. Other types favoured by the USAS were the Bristol F2b for army co-operation, the Bristol Scout for advanced training, the Spad as a fighter and the Caproni for night bombing.

War Department plans proposed an aircraft construction programme of 12,000 machines for 1918 as against the 3,700 put forward by the National Advisory Board for Aeronautics.

> A contract with the French, known as the agreement of August 30, 1917, was prepared and signed by the French Air Ministry and the Commander-in-Chief, AEF. The contract provided that the French Government would deliver to the Air Service, AEF, by June 1, 1918, 5,000 airplanes and 8,500 engines . . . it was upon the provision of this agreement that the Air Service planned its programme of training and of putting squadrons into the field. [*USAS in The First World War*]

It was fully understood that it would be mid 1918 before any appreciable number of American personnel would be ready to join the fray, but some units did become operational in 1917. The first of these was established at a US Naval Air Station on the French coast, using French Le Tellier flying boats for convoy escort work. While American pilots joined training schools in Europe, the command infrastructure was being established for an operational plan that envisaged 190 squadrons by the following July.

The basic organisation of the Air Service, American Expeditionary Force, was set in August 1917 with a Zone of the Interior under Col. R.C. Bolling and a Zone of Advance under Col. William Mitchell (Billy Mitchell of later fame), the overall Chief of the Air Service being Brig.-Gen. William L. Kenly.

Fighter Development

One of the new types to enter operational service with the British was the Sopwith Triplane: the first entered service in the spring of 1917 with the RNAS. The superb manoeuvrability of this aircraft impressed friend and foe. On one of his visits to the front to talk to pilots, Fokker – who, like Geoffrey de Havilland, was keen to obtain first-hand the impressions and opinions at the front-line – was told of the new triplane. This motivated him to look at similar designs using a steel-tube framework.

Then, in July, various German companies were shown a captured Triplane and instructed to produce appropriate designs. This coincided with a report stating that 'the primary task was to procure a new fighter aircraft . . . the Albatros DIII and DV aircraft no longer meet the requirements of the Front for superior fighter aircraft . . . It is essential that the motor industry succeed in producing new power-plants for the D aircraft. They must be more powerful and be produced in large numbers.'

The Fokker Dr1 Triplane entered service in late August 1917, its main advantage over previous types being excellent manoeuvrability. After the initial tests in July, 320 aircraft had been ordered. Its overall speed of 103mph (166kph) was not as good as that of many of its contemporaries and the type suffered reliability problems with the Oberursel engine, as well as certain structural weaknesses. Nevertheless, in the hands of 'higher than average' pilots it soon established a devastating reputation. One of the first to fly the new type operationally was Manfred von Richthofen of JG1 and on 1 September he claimed his first victim (bringing his overall total to 60) with the Triplane by shooting down RE8 B782 of 6 Squadron (Lt. J. Madge and Lt. W. Kember, the latter being killed in the encounter) over Polygon Wood.

The German fighter force was in need of new aircraft, as Richthofen had expressed in mid July:

> You would not believe how low morale is among the fighter pilots presently at the front because of their sorry machines. No-one wants to be a fighter pilot any more . . . We must unconditionally support and use every firm that produces a type somewhat better than this damn Albatros . . . he [Fokker] has a triplane that is certainly no longer in the formative stages and has already shown exceptional climb and speed, that must be unreservedly supported and sent to the Front in large numbers as soon as we have rotary engines.

Like its Sopwith counterpart, the Fokker Triplane was highly manoeuvrable although its overall performance was limited by poor engine performance and lack of reliability.

Appreciation of aerial tactics had also grown as air combats became more frequent and more fierce, and many of the successful fighter pilots made pronouncements on this subject. Richthofen said:

> Every man must have unqualified trust in his leader in the air. If this confidence is lacking then the chances of success are zero. The leader imparts this trust to his Squadron by showing exemplary pluck, being aware of everything, and showing a clear ability to master every situation . . . We don't need aerial acrobats, but men who will go into it with a vengeance . . . For a beginner it is at least equally important to know what he must do to avoid being shot down.

James McCudden, lecturing in August 1917, stated: 'Aerial fighting and tactics have changed very little during the last six months, the only apparent difference being that many more machines are now employed by both sides, and more individual skill in manoeuvring and more general knowledge of tactics appertaining to aerial fighting is shown by both our own and enemy pilots.'

The Summer Offensive

The major Allied attack in the summer took place at Ypres, the offensive being launched on 31 July with massive air support. In the two-week preparation period almost 1,000 enemy batteries had been engaged using air spotting – with an additional 142 by balloon spotting. At the start of the offensive the German air units were outnumbered – 850 aircraft on the Allied side against 600 German – but they had confidence in their equipment and the new fighter organisation of Jastas, most of which were led by charismatic and effective commanders such as Werner Voss. The morale and comradeship of the units was certainly high. It also included the first German fighter wing – Jagdgeschwader 1 (JG) under Manfred von Richthofen, combining Jastas 4, 6, 10 and 11 – with the task of achieving air superiority over whichever sector of the front it was sent to. This élite formation was phenomenally successful but at the cost of robbing other units of their best pilots, and in the face of growing Allied air strength the elite unit could not be everywhere.

The extensive nature of aerial photography is aptly demonstrated by the directive stating that the whole of the Corps area to a depth of 6,500 yards (5,900m) was to be photographed at least twice a week. On a typical day anything up to 1,000 plates might be exposed: the art had come a long way since the primitive visual reports of 1914 and commanders, at all levels, relied on aerial photographs and the maps that were produced from them. It was, of course, similar for all the air arms but the RFC was acknowledged as being the most proficient in this department. The period from 11 to 16 August was particularly active with some 11,000 photographs being taken.

It was now rare for artillery shoots not to include some degree of air spotting – both day and night. One of the most unusual incidents was that of 2 September when a German night artillery co-operation sortie worked with a long-range gun to shell St Omer – over 20 miles behind the lines. The aircraft from 6th Army recorded at least eight direct hits on the target. There was a much greater degree of close air support during this battle than in all those that had gone before. Air power was playing an increasing part in the direct outcome of a battle.

For the French armed forces 1917 was generally a poor year, especially after the disastrous Chemin des Dames offensive, which led to an increased morale problem – even mutinies – among French troops. Part of the problem was the dominance of German air power and the adverse effect that this was having on the front-line troops. Pétain ordered a new policy to be instituted with greater attention being paid

to the 'value of aviation work for troop morale' and that all aviation effort should be concentrated on the land battle.

The most notable event in late September was the death of German ace Lt. Werner Voss. On 23 September he was unfortunate to run into a patrol of seven SE5s from 56 squadron, led by McCudden, who later reported that Voss 'put some bullets through all of our machines. His flying was wonderful, his courage magnificent, and in my opinion he is the bravest German airman whom it has been my privilege to see fight.' Voss fell to the guns of 2nd Lt. Rhys-Davids, one of 56 Squadron's rising stars. At the time of his death, Voss was commander of Jasta 10 and the second highest scoring German pilot, his tally of victories being 48.

Also in September, the first Australian squadron – 69 Squadron, which later became 3 Squadron Australian Flying Corps (AFC) – arrived on the Western Front with RE8s. (The first operational Australian unit had been deployed to the Middle East as early as 1916.)

Attacks on England

By early 1916 some senior German officers were convinced that the airship raids on England would achieve little and that only an aeroplane assault could be effective, especially against London. Such was the view of Generalleutnant von Hoeppner, who proposed a specialist bomber force to be equipped with 30 of the new Gotha G.IV bombers.

In due course Kaghol 1 was ordered to detach three of its squadrons to form the basis of the new Kaghol 3 'Englandgeschwader', which, although attached to the 4th Army, was to report direct to the High Command as a strategic resource. Under its first commander, Hpt. Ernst Brandenburg, it was ordered to 'disrupt the British war industry, disorganise the communications between coastal ports and hinder the transport of war materials across the Channel.'

The strategic campaign against England by the Zeppelins had proved expensive and ineffective towards the end of 1917 but the new year saw the Germans with new plans and an unprecedented determination to take the war to the enemy homeland. While their airships continued to play a part in this offensive, it was strategic bombing aeroplanes that now came to the fore

and led to the period being known as the 'Gotha Summer'.

The Zeppelins had returned to London on the night of 16/17 March, five airships causing minimal damage as poor weather had caused a dispersion of effort. However, Kaghol 3 was now well advanced with its work-up for its strategic offensive, despite continued problems with the D.IVa engines of the Gothas. The unit moved, in April, to new bases at St Denis-Westrem and Mariakerke, two Staffeln each of six Gotha G.IVs going to each location. The first raid was launched on 25 May when 23 aircraft left their bases for Nieuwmunster to refuel. At around 5pm, two formations of bombers (a total of 21 aircraft) crossed the Essex coast between the Blackwater and Crouch estuaries. Bad weather near Gravesend forced the leader to turn south and attack secondary targets such as Lympne and Folkestone. Despite being deflected from the intended target, it was a very successful first outing for the new unit – they had cruised over England for well over an hour with virtually no opposition.

They were, however, intercepted on the return journey by RNAS Pups and Triplanes from the Dunkirk area; although the pilots claimed to have shot down two of the bombers, German records show the that only one crashed as a result of this engagement and one other was damaged. In view of this fighter threat, Brandenburg requested that a fighter escort should meet the returning bombers on future operations.

The raid certainly generated heated discussion in the War Office, for although quite a number of defensive sorties were flown only two aircraft were able to close with the bombers – and both proved ineffective. It was to be no better on 5 June when the Gothas returned, even though this coincided with a practice alert that meant that the Home Defence force was even more prepared than usual! Some 60 aircraft scrambled to seek the raiders, who had again abandoned plans to reach London and had gone for secondary targets on the coast. Gotha '660 crashed into the sea – probably as a result of anti-aircraft fire – but the remaining aircraft had no trouble until they were engaged by the RNAS aircraft from bases in the Dunkirk area. The German fighter escorts were able to prevent the British fighters from closing with the bombers, although the RNAS pilots claimed to have shot down three of the fighters. (In the same month the

German Army abolished its airship service and transferred the remaining airships to the Navy, whose faith in the type still remained strong.)

It was only on the third aeroplane raid, on 13 June, that the bombers managed to reach London: 16 aircraft delivered an attack that caused heavy damage and high casualties. Despite 79 defensive sorties being flown, all the Gothas returned safely and the battle seemed to be going in favour of the bombers. While the British pondered ways of redressing the balance, the Germans celebrated and Brandenburg was awarded the 'Blue Max' – though this proved to be a tragedy for the unit as he was injured in an accident on the way back from the ceremony and the command of Kaghol 3 went to the more impetuous Hpt. Rudolf Kleine.

Meanwhile, the British came up with a two-pronged attempt to defeat the bombers – attack their bases and strengthen the Home Defence force, even at the expense of the Western Front. Revenge attacks were also being considered. On 17 June Trenchard commented: 'reprisals on open towns are repugnant to British ideas, but we may be forced to adopt them . . . at present we are not prepared to carry out reprisals effectively, being unprovided with suitable machines.' It was decided to re-deploy two experienced fighter squadrons from the Western Front, 56 squadron going to Bekesbourne and 66 Squadron to the Calais area (although these units were returned to their original duties by early July).

Another effective attack on London on 7 July caused the same arguments to be raised but with no firm conclusions being reached. In a statement to Parliament, Prime Minister Lloyd George said: 'The first consideration before the Government is to see that the Army in France is sufficiently supplied with aeroplanes. A sufficiency of aeroplanes means everything to that Army. They are the eyes of the Army, which cannot advance without them.' This statement shows that the first consideration was still that of reconnaissance. Nevertheless, some positive moves were taken, such as diverting Camels from delivery to France in order to equip 44 Squadron at Hainault Farm.

Bad weather kept the Gothas inactive for the next few weeks but on 12 August Kleine decided to ignore weather warnings and deliver another blow to London. Although 13 aircraft took off, three had to turn back with engine problems (the Gotha engines continued to be troublesome). The

re-organized air defence network in southern England responded quickly and in force, some 134 aircraft being sent up. The net result was that two of the Gothas were shot down by fighters and others damaged. The weather conditions over the Continent were, as forecast, poor and in the gathering dusk and blustery conditions, four of the Gothas crashed while trying to land.

It was the same on 18 August when a large raid of 28 Gothas took off but were forced to turn back before crossing the coast of England. Their attempt to return home was a disaster, as four aircraft crashed in the sea, one was shot down over Holland, two force-landed in Holland and four others force-landed when they ran out of fuel. The remainder landed in 'a series of controlled crashes'.

Despite such catastrophes, the potential of strategic bombing was being seen by a number of air arms; on 17 August the Smuts Report included the comment that: 'Unlike artillery, an air fleet can conduct extensive operations far from, and independent of, both Army and Navy. As far as can at present be foreseen, there is absolutely no limit to the scale of its future war use.'

While the War Office considered this and other similar comments – which would in due course lead to the formation of the Royal Air Force and, within that, the Independent Force (a strategic bombing force) – the Gothas suffered another blow. Of 15 aircraft that set out on 22 August, two were shot down by fighters (of which 136 were airborne) and one by anti-aircraft fire. Even then, their problems were not over and the returning bombers were intercepted by fighters from France. The German fighter escort appeared on the scene and a major air battle ensued, during which the RNAS flyers claim to have driven down five of their opposite number. Only seven Gothas returned home and all were damaged. In the face of such determined and effective opposition the Gothas abandoned their daylight campaign and turned to night bombing.

The night offensive began in September, the first raid being flown on 2/3 September when aircraft of Kaghol 4 attacked Dover. Two nights later 11 bombers aimed for London, although only five claim to have attacked the target; one bomber was shot down by anti-aircraft fire. On 24 September there was the launch of what was known as the 'Harvest Moon offensive' and over the period to 2 October a series of raids were flown, including six to London. Loss rates

remained high: 13 bombers out of 92 were lost to a variety of causes. On occasion these attacks were part of a combined offensive with Zeppelins, such had been the case on 24/25 September when the airships attacked targets in the Midlands while their aeroplane colleagues went for London.

However, the most significant development was the introduction to the campaign of the 'R-planes', the first two joining a raid on 28/29 September. The R-type (R standing for Riesenflugzeug or 'giant aeroplane') had its origin as early as 1914 when prototype VGO I had its first flight. However, it was over a year before the first R-plane saw operational service, the SSW R.1 being attached to FA 31 at Slonium on the Eastern Front. However, it saw no action due to a series of technical problems and it was not until the following August that the first truly operational units were employed.

RFa 500 operated the VGO II and III on the Eastern Front, the first attack being made on 13 August against rail facilities in Estonia. Although little use was made of these aircraft, the operational experience was valuable and as new R-planes, with better reliability and performance, became available, then the potential looked reasonable. By July 1917 RFa 501 was at Berlin training on the Staaken R.VI. Although only 18 of these aircraft were produced, the type was one of the most successful 'strategic bombers' of the war. In August RFa 501 moved to Belgium ready for their operational debut.

The bomber attack on England was assisted by the ineffectiveness of many of the existing Home Defence aircraft. With the previous concept that single-seat fighters were not suitable for night operations, plus the need for as many as possible of these types on the Western Front, there was little that could be done to improve the situation. However, the earlier decision to equip 44 Squadron with Camels, and the determined leadership of that unit by the experienced night fighter pilot, Murlis Green, were to pay dividends. The night raids continued and at last, on the night of 18/19 December, flying Camel B5192 from Hainault, Green managed to shoot down one of the Gotha raiders.

Autumn Battles in Flanders

After the mud of Passchendaele in October and early November, the final part of the Ypres offensive in late November saw the

British 3rd Army launch an offensive at Cambrai, the theory being that German attention and strength was concentrated in Flanders. New tactics were employed with a mass of tanks providing the 'punch' rather than a heavy artillery bombardment. The RFC squadrons were intended to provide their usual intense air cover and support but for the first few days of the attack this was limited by poor weather. However, they were soon in action providing valuable help to tanks that were being held up by German anti-tank gun positions. The Germans were not as weak as was expected and the British recoiled in the face of a counter-attack launched on 30 November.

The German trench strafers also were out in force, operating from airfields close to the front and using machine guns, grenades and fragmentation bombs to cause havoc among the Allied infantry. Most attacks were delivered from less than 200ft (60m) and it was only the armour plate on the aircraft that prevented crippling losses to ground fire.

On 27 November Brig.-Gen. Benjamin D. Foulis took over as head of the Air Service, AEF, and the following month he sent a memo to the Chief of Staff:

The British and French authorities have fully appreciated the importance of a strategic air offensive against German industrial centres and lines of communication, bet they have never been able to provide enough personnel and airplanes to take care of the tactical air units with troops and also provide additional units for strategic offensive operations. Our entry into the war with large resources of personnel and aircraft materials, if promptly taken advantage of, will allow the Allies and ourselves to take the strategic offensive next summer against German industrial centres, German airdromes and German lines-of-communication.

Trenchard later summarized his thoughts on French aviation at this period, saying that it 'excels in conception but fails in execution.' This was a fairly widely held view and although the French air service was strong in numbers and included superb fighter types – and a number of outstanding individual units – it was considered that the overall effectiveness of French aviation was lower than it should have been.

Aircraft and aero engine production had increased markedly for all the major belligerents, the German war industry having achieved a figure of almost 1,000 aircraft a month. But there were still significant problems, especially in America where attempts to adapt some of the Allied types were proving troublesome. For German industry the winter of 1917/18 was to bring major problems through a lack of essential supplies such as coal. The removal of Russia from the war gave new heart to the Germans but most appreciated that they would have only one chance to secure victory before the sheer weight of American military power would have a decisive effect – the spring of 1918 was to be critical for both sides.

A significant event of 1917 was of course the departure of Russia from the war. Air power was never a major factor on the Eastern Front: at the beginning of 1917 the Russians had an air strength of just over 500 aircraft, of which over 100 were Nieuports, but they were completely dominated by the German air units both in quality and numbers. The Russian Naval Air Service had grown only slowly and had only just over 100 aircraft, 35 of which were flying-boats – the best and most effective being the Grigorovich types, operating over the Baltic and Black Sea.

The German naval aviators were also active. Lt. Wolfram Eisenlohr was an observer on seaplanes operating over the Baltic: 'In 1917 we finally received 60kg bombs. It was one of these bombs that on August 22, 1917 I used to sink the Russian destroyer *Stroini*. We attacked the Russian vessels with three twin-engine FF41As. In the nose of the aircraft there was a big open 'balcony' where the observer sat. As soon as we neared the target, the pilot, who sat behind me, could no longer see the object of the attack. Thus, my duty as observer was to signal the pilot, Oblt Gruder, and to drop the bombs at the right time.'

Eisenlohr continued: 'Before us lay two Russian destroyers. The observer of the preceding aircraft dropped four bombs on each one, I followed the four bombs and saw that each one hit closer and closer to the ship, but that the last detonated about 10m ahead of it. I then considered that if I were to toss all eight bombs one right after the other, the probability of a hit would be substantial. The fifth bomb was actually a hit. It struck the *Stroini* in a sensitive part and caused it to sink.' [Wolfram Eisenlohr, *Cross & Cockade International*, Vol. 25/1]

It was the land war that decided events. Increasing discontent among the troops, under the influence of Communist agitators, was a major factor in the Russian revolution. When the Bolsheviks seized power from the Provisional Government of Kerensky in November, Lenin quickly came to terms with the Germans and the war was over. The air elements of the German armed forces could, and did, move west quickly to reinforce their colleagues on the Western Front; the mass of ground forces would take longer to re-organize and transport.

Other Theatres

The war against Turkey entered a phase of almost continual Allied advances and the squadrons in this theatre provided invaluable assistance to all aspects of the Allied operations. There were instances when the impact of air power was decisive. Such was the case during the second Gaza offensive in April. On 20 April, reconnaissance observed a Turkish force of 2,000 infantry and 800 cavalry gathering for a counterstroke and so a bomber force (of only four aircraft) was sent to attack. The result was that 'the whole force was scattered in all directions, and when our pilots left, the cavalry was still galloping eastwards. As a result, the enemy attack on our right flank failed to materialise.'

In October the Palestine Brigade was formed to command all RFC units east of the Suez Canal, a total of four squadrons. Gen. Allenby planned his autumn offensive with great care and the Third Battle of Gaza opened on 31 October with Beersheba as the main target. By 7 November the Turks were in retreat and much of the Gaza Line had fallen: 'special photographic maps were made, and a continuous supply of these were provided to the Corps concerned, either by air or special messenger.'

At this point the RFC was given freedom to disrupt and harass the retreating enemy, a task that they performed with startling success. Typical of the attacks during this phase was that of 9 November when 22 aircraft attacked El Tine, the railhead and depot of the Turkish 8th Army, causing serious damage. According to a German report 'this did more to break the heart of the Eighth Army and to diminish its fighting strength than all the hard fighting that had gone before.' By early December other crucial areas such as Jaffa, Lydda (now Lod) and Jerusalem had also been lost by the Turks.

It was a similar story in Mesopotamia: small numbers of aircraft but significant impact on events. During the months before the capture of Baghdad on 3 March air co-operation was developed to the fullest extent, and incessant attacks were made on the enemy both in the air and on the ground . . . exhaustive reports were made on the disposition of his forces, gun-pits and trenches, and photographs were taken of the whole of the Tigris as far as Baghdad, from which all maps were complied . . . owing to the scattered disposition of the enemy forces, and the great distance of these from Baghdad, the General Staff had to rely almost entirely on aeroplanes for quick and accurate information regarding his movements.

The Turkish army was in retreat in most areas and their air elements, even when supported by German aircraft, played little part in events.

The Salonica front was the only one in which the hard-pressed Turks were given significant air assets by their German allies and early in 1917 a powerful bombing force was moved from Bucharest in order to make attacks on the British and French positions. Typical of the attacks made by this mixed bomber force was that of 27 February when 20 aircraft attacked Salonica. They were intercepted by 17 Squadron and in the ensuing combat the bomber force was forced to scatter and one Halberstadt forced to land. The arrival of better aircraft types, such as the SE5a, Camel and Bristol monoplanes 'marked the beginning of air superiority for the RFC on this front which was maintained, with an ever-increasing effectiveness, until the end.' [AP125]

In German East Africa the campaign against Gen. von Lettow Vorbeck continued in June with the RFC's 26 Squadron supporting the ground forces, along with a number of RNAS aeroplanes. The German retreat into Portuguese East Africa towards the end of the year brought operations to a close and most Allied air assets gathered at Mtua.

In Italy the Isonzo remained the focus of attention throughout the year and it was here that most of the fighting, ground and air, took place. The Austro-Hungarian squadrons were increasingly deprived of German aircraft as the year wore on, the latter being unable to spare effective combat types to help their ally. But their own manufacturers, such as Brandenburg, were increasing production and providing a steady flow of good aircraft. Likewise, the Italian air elements grew slowly in numbers and effectiveness. Much attention was paid to offensive operations by bombers and in support of ground forces.

During the 10th battle of the Isonzo in May, sorties were flown by up to 40 Caproni bombers in direct support of infantry attacks. Although little material damage appears to have been done, it did have a significant effect on morale – for both sides. Similarly on 19 August, the first day of the 11th Isonzo, 85 Capronis escorted by over 100 fighters supported the infantry attack and continued to do so for the next ten days. Italian bombing was effective and determined, but costly – 81 Caproni aircrew were lost during this ten-day period. Defeat at the 12th Isonzo in October led to use of the bombers to try and stem the Austrian advance. They were partly successful, again at the price of high casualties.

Following this defeat at Caporetto, the Allies sent reinforcements. The air element comprised ten French and five British squadron, the latter being the RFC's VII Brigade equipped with RE8s and Camels. The squadrons became operational on 29 November and were soon involved in the range of missions that some of them had become used to on the Western Front, in the face of extensive enemy air activity air combat was frequent and in the period up to the end of December they claimed 13 aircraft shot down and a further six driven down out of control, against the loss of two of their own number.

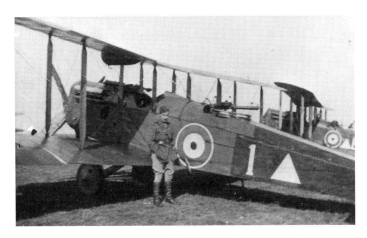

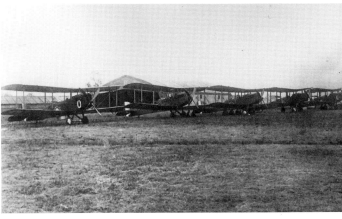

Above left: The first operational unit with the DH4 was 55 Squadron, from January 1917. The unit moved to France in March and was soon heavily engaged on reconnaissance and bombing. In October the Squadron joined the newly formed 41st Wing as part of a new strategic bombing force to attack targets in Germany. (Peter Green Collection)

Above right: The RNAS also used the DH4, the first unit being 2 (Naval) Squadron at St Pol in March 1917. This unit specialized in reconnaissance and artillery spotting for naval monitors. The type also served with the RNAS in the Mediterranean theatre. (Peter Green Collection)

Above: Early 1917 saw another batch of Squadrons join the RFC in France as air strength continued to increase. This shot shows 48 Squadron at Rendcombe in March, just prior to their departure to France as the first Bristol Fighter Squadron. (Ken Delve Collection)

Right: 43 Squadron took its Sopwith 1½ Strutters to France in January for fighter-reconnaissance duties, operating initially from Treizennes. This view of A1052 is either at that field or at Auchel, where the Squadron moved in May. (Peter Green Collection)

Right: The Armstrong Whitworth FK8 was designed as a two-seat reconnaissance-bomber. Powered by a 160hp Beardmore, the type had a speed of just under 100mph (160kph) and a ceiling of 13,000ft (4,000m). (Ken Delve Collection)

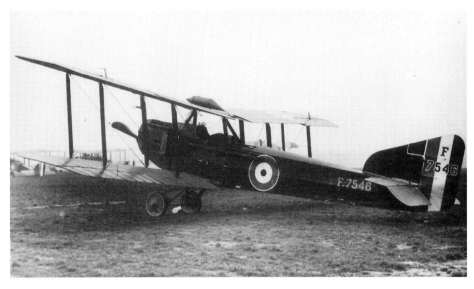

Left: The FK8 had reasonable handling qualities and entered operational service in France with 35 Squadron in January 1917. The RFC prided itself on the determination with which it achieved its reconnaissance task – regardless of the air opposition – and the FK8 played a leading role in this. (Ken Delve Collection)

Right: Although it looked somewhat ungainly, the FK8's performance was average for reconnaissance-bomber aircraft of the period – but far below that of the fighters, making it vulnerable if not escorted. (*FlyPast* Collection)

Opposite page: **FK8 C8550 of 2 Squadron, a unit that operated the type from April 1917 to beyond the end of the war. It was while flying one of these aircraft that Capt. F. West became involved in a dramatic air battle with German fighters and won the Victoria Cross.** (Ken Delve Collection)

Right: **Checking out the aircraft ready for another sortie – an FK8 crew; good view of the Lewis gun with its simple ring-and-bead sight.** (Ken Delve Collection)

Left: **Thousands of photographs, obliques and verticals were taken by RFC aircraft; this 2 Squadron shot shows a kite balloon. These balloons were major elements in the artillery co-ordination network and Allied pilots devoted much effort to their destruction.** (Ken Delve Collection)

Below: **The German submarines were a major problem for Allied shipping around the UK and the RNAS's flying boats, such as this FBA, flew thousands of hours on anti-submarine patrols. The FBA (Franco-British Aviation) was a small two-seat aircraft of which some 128 were used by the RNAS.** (Capt. D.S. Glover)

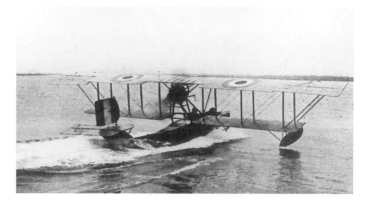

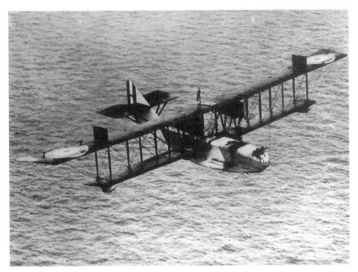

Above left: **Felixstowe F2A on patrol being flown by Acting Flt. Cdr. R.D. Delamere.** (Jack Bruce/Stuart Leslie collection)

Above right: **1917 saw the appearance of a number of triplane designs; the Sopwith Triplane was adopted by the RNAS as its superb manoeuvrability and top speed of 113mph (182kph) made it an excellent fighter – even though most were armed only with a single Vickers gun. N5351, a Clayton & Shuttleworth example, is seen here at Cranwell in February 1917 but it was soon operational with 8 Squadron RNAS.** (Peter Green Collection)

Right: **Another of the Sopwith Triplane users, 10 Squadron RNAS. This squadron had formed at St Pol in February 1917, initially with the Nieuport 12.** (Harry Holmes)

Left: **The French accepted a limited number of Sopwith Triplanes, this example being with the Naval Fighter Flight at St Pol in 1917.** (Andy Thomas Collection)

Right: **Pup A674 is seen here with 66 Squadron, this unit having re-equipped in March 1917 and moved to France as one of the new fighter units.** (Ken Delve Collection)

Left: **The Sopwith Scout (or Pup as it was more generally known) served with the RFC and RNAS as an effective fighter from late 1916 and was an important type during the air battles of 1917; '9902 is a Beardmore-built example.** (Harry Holmes)

Below: **Powered by a Le Rhône, the Pup equipped a number of RNAS units as well as RFC squadrons on the Western Front and for Home Defence. A6231 is here with 73 Squadron at Lilbourne in summer 1917; the Squadron was equipped with Sopwith Camels and moved to France early in 1918.** (Ken Delve Collection)

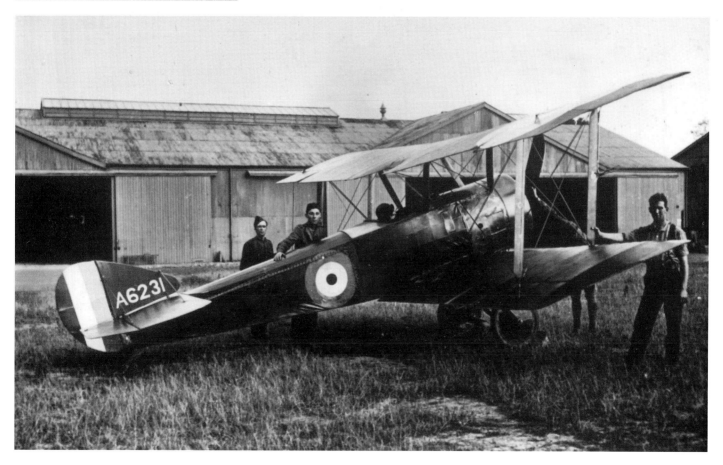

Left: RE7 '2194 with 35 Reserve Squadron at Northolt in 1917; this aircraft was one of a batch of 50 built by the Coventry Ordnance Works. (Capt. D.S. Glover)

Right: Demonstrating the operation of a camera fitted to the RE8. The primary role of the aircraft was reconnaissance and during its operational career many thousands of plates were exposed – a vital contribution to Allied military planning. (Capt. D.S. Glover)

Right: **RE8 of 52 Squadron.** (Jack Bruce/Stuart Leslie collection)

Left: **With its Presentation inscription 'New South Wales No 15', DH5 A9197 was one of several such aircraft to serve with 68 Squadron (later to become 2 Squadron Australian Flying Corps). Production of the DH5 fighter commenced in early 1917 but it was the summer before any significant numbers were available.** (Peter Green Collection)

Right: **The Airco DH6 was designed to be a reliable and straightforward trainer, with ease of manufacture and maintenance as the two prime considerations. Production began early in 1917 and very large numbers were ordered from a variety of contractors. Most of the reserve and training units used the type at some time. A9644 is shown with 23rd Training Wing at Scampton.** (Peter Green Collection)

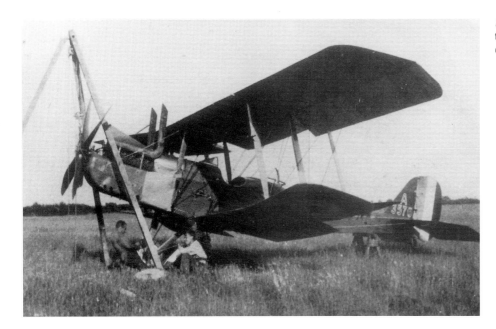

Left: **Recovery work on RE8 A3570 at Wyton in May 1917; the tripod lifting tackle was both easy to transport and effective.** (Capt. D .S. Glover)

Right: **Seen at Hounslow sometime in 1917 is FE9 A4818; it has extensive graffiti around the forward fuselage but this is unfortunately unreadable. Designed as a two-seat fighter-reconnaissance replacement for the FE2b, the type arrived in France in the summer of 1917 for trials but in the event was only produced in limited numbers.** (Capt. D.S. Glover)

Left: **Meanwhile, the FE2b soldiered on although with the increasing numbers of better aircraft available from early 1917 it was soon 'relegated' to the night bomber role – as here with A4578 of 100 Squadron, this unit having formed in February 1917 for this specific role with the FE2b.** (Peter Green Collection)

Right: **100 Squadron FE2b in its night environment, Western Front 1917. Note the underwing bracket for the 'Holt' landing flare.** (Ken Delve Collection)

Left: **58 Squadron personnel, July 1917 – towards the end of the year the squadron re-equipped with FE2bs to join the night offensive, eventually carrying out its first raid on 2 February 1918.** (Ken Delve Collection)

Right: **By 1917 the RFC had identified the need for a specialist day bomber aircraft – especially in response to the growing degree of such activity by the Germans. The longer range of the proposed DH9 persuaded the Air Board to place orders for the type and by late 1917 it was under test at Martlesham. C2228 here was with 31 TS at Fowlmere in late 1918.** (Capt. D.S. Glover)

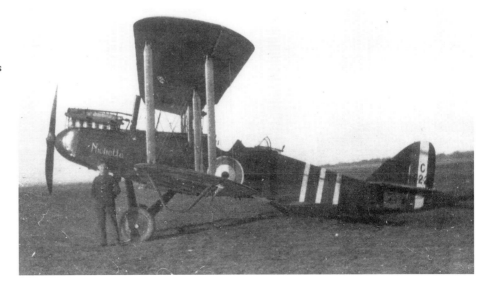

Left: **With a number of Spad-like features, the Vickers FB16 fighter was designed around the Hart radial engine, although following problems with this it was given a 150hp Hispano-Suiza and appeared as the FB.16D. Pilots such as James McCudden (in June 1917) were impressed: 'at 10,000ft it was 30 mph faster at least than anything I had yet flown.' However, this promising type was not put into production.** (Peter Green Collection)

Right: **New fighters under design in 1916 began to make their appearance; SE5 prototype A4561 had first flown in November 1916 and the following month was in France for pilot evaluation. It was generally well liked but there were problems, some of which had not been resolved when the first production aircraft were delivered in March 1917.** (Harry Holmes)

Below: **56 Squadron SE5 A4863 at London Colney in April 1917, before leaving for France. As the first SE5 unit, 56 Squadron received aircraft from March 1917 and the following month moved to France.** (Jack Bruce/Stuart Leslie collection)

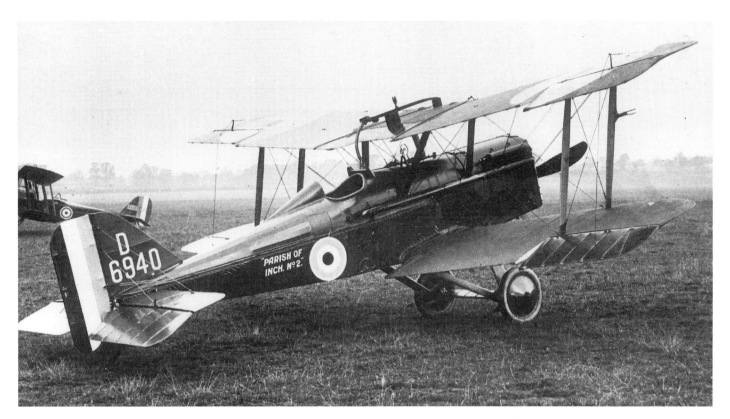

Above: The SE5a was one of the classic British fighters and was a direct follow-on from the SE5; the type entered service in the spring of 1917 and, despite a number of engine problems, was an immediate success. (Peter Green Collection)

Right: Aircraft of the second SE5 production batch were given the larger windscreen – giving a semi-enclosed cockpit – but this was not liked by the operational pilots as it was thought to be too restrictive. A8904 is see here at Farnborough in April 1917; it subsequently became operational with 56 Squadron and flew its first combat patrol on **May 6.** (Harry Holmes)

Right: Unidentified SE5a fitted with a four-bladed propeller normally found on machines with the geared Hispano-Suiza V-8 engine. (Ken Delve Collection)

Left: **The RNAS also acquired the Camel. This aircraft, N6336, was delivered to Martlesham for engine tests in May 1917 as it was one of a small batch with a 150hp BR.1. It was later operational with a number of units until, in October 1917, it became a Ground Instructional airframe.** (Capt. D.S. Glover)

Right: **Camp Bray Dunes May 1917, home to 4 Squadron RNAS and a French unit.** (IWM Q69454)

Below left: **The Nieuport 17bis differed from the 17/23 (those two types being virtually indistinguishable) in its circular fuselage and the use of a Clerget engine in place of the normal 110hp Le Rhone.** (Peter Green Collection)

Below right: **The stringers making up the circular shape of this Nieuport 17bis, N1895, can be clearly seen.** (Ken Wixey Collection)

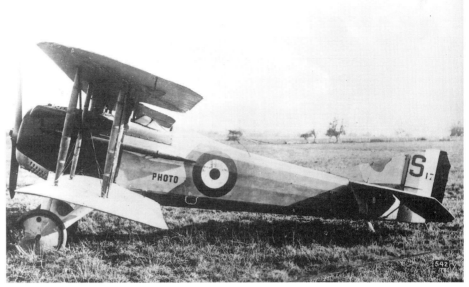

Above left: **Lt. Gilbert Sardier. At the age of 21 he was in command of SPA 48.** (Dennis Hylands)

Above right: **The Spad VII was the favoured mount of many of the French aces.** (Ken Wixey Collection)

Centre right: **Spad VII of** *Les Cignones* **at Dunkirk in 1917.** (Jack Bruce/Stuart Leslie collection)

Right: **Nieuport 24 N3961 of Escadrille N91; the type was not a great success in view of the increasing availability of superior Spad fighters.** (Jean Devaux)

Left: The two-seat Spad XI was conceived as a reconnaissance-bomber but following its introduction in 1917 was not a great success. Nevertheless, it was delivered in large numbers and continued in use until mid 1918. (MAP)

Right: The Morane-Saulnier Type A was designed in 1917 and over 1,200 of the type were built, the introduction to service being in September. However, it had only three months operational service before being withdrawn for training use on the grounds that the engine was unreliable and better types were becoming available. (MAP)

Left: Morane-Saulnier A1 '1543; the type had an impressive top speed of 138mph (222kph) and was a potent machine. (Ken Wixey Collection)

Above: **SPA 103 – one of the greatest of French fighter units. Ace René Fonck is in the centre of this photo.** (Dennis Hylands)

Right: **Rugged and dependable, and rated amongst the top three fighters of the War, the Spad VII served on to the end of the war.** (Ken Wixey Collection)

Left: **The Halberstadt CLII was one of the types built in 1917 for Schützstaffeln (escort flights) – a two-seat fighter escort armed with one or two Spandaus plus a parabellum for the observer.** (MAP)

Left: With the growing importance of providing close support for the infantry, especially during an attack, a number of aircraft were given such close air support as their main role – such was the case with the Halberstadt CLII and here a crew of Schlachstaffel 27 is seen loading weapons onto the aircraft. (Alex Imrie)

Centre right: **Albatros DIII having been recovered by the Allies and in the process of being repaired. The type began its combat career over the Western Front in early 1917 and by the spring was taking an increasing toll of Allied aircraft. The term 'Albatros Nieuport' refers to its Nieuport-like sesquiplane wing layout.** (Capt. D.S. Glover)

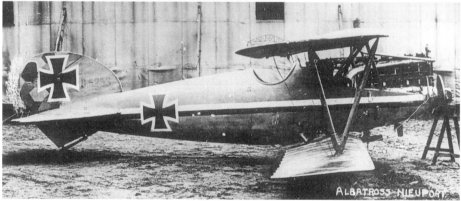

Below right: **The Albatros DV entered service in May 1917 to counter British types such as the SE5; although it was not as promising as expected, it was still ordered in large numbers and remained in use to the end of the war. Powered by a 180hp or 200hp Mercedes DIIIa it had a top speed of 116mph (187kph).** (MAP)

Right: **Jasta 26 in April 1917; Royal Prussian Jagdstaffel 26 was formed on 14 December 1916 and was operational in late January under Oblt Bruno Loerzer, who held command through to February 1918. The Jasta was credited with 180 victories by the end of the war.** (IWM Q69207)

Left: **The Roland DV was one of a number of designs for which only a single prototype was built in 1917, a period when the Germans were searching for new fighter designs to develop to counter the growing numbers and capabilities of Allied designs.** (MAP)

Below: **The DFW CV was another type involved with ground support missions.** (Ken Delve Collection)

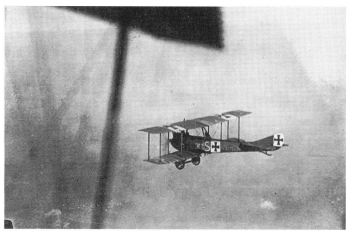

Above left: **An Ufag-built Brandenburg CI in Poland mid 1917; over 1,200 of this type were built for use by the Austrians and Ufag contributed over 700 of these.** (*FlyPast* Collection)

Above right: **The Aviatik BII had been phased out of operational use but was still in use with training schools – as shown by the 'S' on the airframe of this example.** (*Freitag*)

Above: **Summer 1917 and crews pose with an Albatros CI; although the type had entered service in 1915 as a general-purpose aircraft it had by 1917 been relegated to other uses. A dual-control trainer variant was also in use.** (*Freitag*)

Right: **A well wrapped-up crew in their Albatros CVI – Lt. Bassenge and Uffz. Flöel. Open-air cockpits, winter conditions and high flying combined to make aircraft in the First World War quite uncomfortable!** (Plickert)

Right: **Gen. von Hoeppner visiting Schleissheim in mid 1917; three Fokker DVs and one Fokker DIII are in the line.** (Alex Imrie)

Below: **An impressive line-up of Albatros fighters.** (*FlyPast* Collection)

Right: **The Fokker Dr1 was, despite its obvious failings, well liked by many of the pilots, a number of whom were reluctant to trade in their mounts even when technically superior fighters became available. It was one of those aircraft that acquired a mystique, a mystique that still survives today!** (*FlyPast* Collection)

Above: **Fokker Dr1 403/17 of JG1 with Lt. Janzen.** (Alex Imrie)

Above: **This Richthofen portrait shows Maj. Albrecht von Richthofen flanked by Manfred (on his left) and Lothar.** (Ken Delve Collection)

Below: **Manfred von Richthofen (centre) with squadron pilots. The 'Red Baron' finally met his death in combat having scored 80 victories – the top-scoring pilot of the First World War.** (Ken Delve Collection)

Above left: **When triplanes seemed to hold the most promise as fighters a number of designs were put forward. This Albatros Dr1 was built in 1917 – and as can be clearly seen it was essentially an Albatros DV with an extra wing added.** (MAP)

Above right: **Curtiss JN-4 of the RFC's Training Brigade in Canada.** (Ken Delve Collection)

Right: **No 4 School of Military Aeronautics formed in Canada during the first half of 1917 to increase the training output. Curtiss JN-4 C245 has suffered the fate of many a training aircraft – but fortunately the crews often escaped without injury.** (Ken Delve Collection)

Below: **In addition to the standard flying training schools, a number of specialist establishments formed. This shot of August 1917 shows instructors and mechanics of No 1 School of Special Flying at Gosport; the school had formed that month to train instructors. Its effect on flying training as a whole is still felt today.** (Harry Holmes)

Above: **Avro 504 A8515 at Harling Road; the Avro 504 series saw limited operational employment but extensive use as training aircraft throughout the war.** (Capt. D.S. Glover)

Above: **The Avro 504J, with its 80hp Le Rhône or 100hp Gnome Monosoupape, entered service in the summer of 1917. With light yet powerful controls and capable of full aerobatics, the 504J was a superb training machine. This is a School of Special Flying example at Gosport.** (*FlyPast* Collection)

Below: **An RFC aerial photograph of the German airfield at Gontrode on 5 September 1917. This was one of the bases of the German strategic bombing force.** (Peter Green Collection)

Above: Gotha GIV being manhandled. This was one of the main variants of the Gotha bomber series and became part of the German strategic bombing offensive in 1917. The aircraft carried a crew of three, with two parabellums for self defence and a bomb load of up to 1,100lb (500kg). (Hoppe)

Above: Kaghol 3's Gotha GIVs at Nieuwmunster in May 1917; the bombers used this airfield as a refuelling stop when mounting attacks on England. (Alex Imrie)

Right: The Staaken RVI was the most prolific of the giant 'R' planes with 18 built. They saw service on the Western Front from mid 1917, the first raid against England being on 17 September. (MAP)

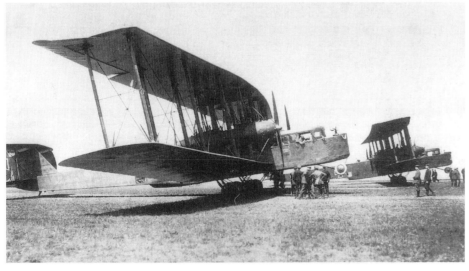

Left: Two Staaken RVI bombers – 36/16 and 33/16 of RFa 501. (Ken Delve Collection)

Left: **LZ113**, one of the later series of 'Super Zeppelins'. By 1918 the Home Defence organization in Britain would be too powerful and the night raids by airships generally ineffective and costly. (Ken Wixey Collection)

Right: **Even the famous Zeppelin-killing 39 Squadron was having to manage with outdated equipment: note the black-painted BE12 in the hangar behind the pilot group at North Weald.** (G.S. Leslie)

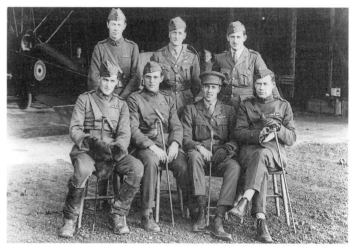

Below: **The Home Defence units were still equipped with a range of types, most of which were unable to deal with the new German bombers and super-Zeppelins. The BE2c was still on strength with a number of Squadrons – as here in 58 Squadron's hangar at Cramlington.** (Ken Delve Collection)

Right: **Another type to join the night battle was the FE2b, seen here with 51 Squadron**. (Ken Delve Collection)

Left: **With its twin upward-firing guns, Sopwith 1½ Strutter B762 was one of a number of such aircraft employed for Home Defence in a single-seat form. It served with 78 Squadron from the autumn of 1917, having replaced BE2 and BE12 variants.** (Peter Green Collection)

Right: **With the growth of the daylight bombing threat, fighter types joined the Home Defence force – as here with Sopwith 1½ Strutter A8274 in service with 37 Squadron in mid 1917. The Squadron occupied four LGs in Essex, the prime area over which the Gothas flew to reach their targets.** (Peter Green Collection)

Left: It was not only the dedicated Home Defence Squadrons that took part in the battle; other units sent aircraft up. On 22 August Flt. Lt. A. Brandon was flying Camel B3834, from the War Flight at Manston, when he attacked a number of Gothas; of the 10 aircraft on the raid, three were shot down by anti-aircraft and aeroplane attacks, and Brandon was involved in at least one of these victories. The 'Wonga Bonga' graphic refers to the noise that the Gotha engines made. (Peter Green Collection)

Right: The high-flying Rumplers were effective German reconnaissance aircraft as they were able to escape most attackers by taking advantage of the ceiling of 21,000ft (6,400m). (MAP)

Left: Captured AGO GIV; the unique tapering wings, not particularly clear in this view, made the aircraft distinctive. The type was active as a two-seat reconnaissance aircraft in small numbers during 1917. (MAP)

Right: **Hannover CLII. Dubbed 'Hannoveranas' by the RFC, they entered operational service towards the end of 1917 and proved to be an effective two-seat fighter, often used in the escort role.** (Ken Delve Collection)

Left: **The Halberstadt CLII was increasingly used by the 'battle flights' for trench warfare; armed with machine guns, bombs and hand-grenades the aircraft flew very low, attacking ground troops and causing havoc.** (MAP)

Right: **The Fokker Triplane, FI 103/17 of Werner Voss, one of the leading fighter pilots during 1917. His career started in November 1916 with Jasta 2 and by the following summer he had 30 victories and was commanding Jasta 10.** (Ken Delve Collection)

Left: **Pfalz DIII 1370/17 (which acquired G.110 as its captured serial). The aircraft belonged to Jasta 10 and was shot down by a 35 Squadron aircraft on 27 December 1917. It is seen here at Estrées-aux-Chausée.** (Peter Green Collection)

Left: **By November 1917 there were well over 400 Albatros DIIIs in front-line service, although by the summer the types had been technologically superseded by the DV.** (Ken Delve Collection)

Right: **This angle clearly shows the upper wing cut-out on this Albatros DIII to improve the pilot's forward and upward view and the smooth, semi-monocoque plywood fuselage.** (Dennis Hylands)

Right: **The Albatros DV was a follow-on to the successful DIII in response to the improvements in Allied fighter types; it entered service in May 1917 and by mid summer was appearing in increasing numbers. This captured example is formerly 1102/17 and is seen at Lympne in August 1917.** (Capt. D.S. Glover)

Left: **The Pfalz DIII reached the Bavarian units at the front in the autumn of 1917. An Allied test on an aircraft captured the following February praised most aspects of this fighter.** (Ken Delve Collection)

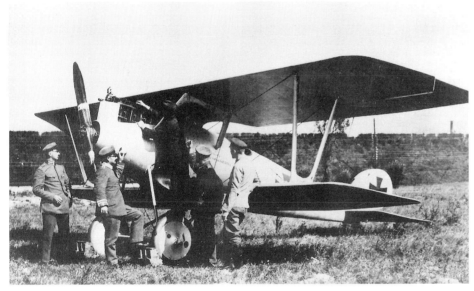

Right: **Gen. Ludendorff visited Courtrai on 18 August 1917 to review Jasta 2; one of the unit's Albatros DVs is in the background.** (Ken Delve Collection)

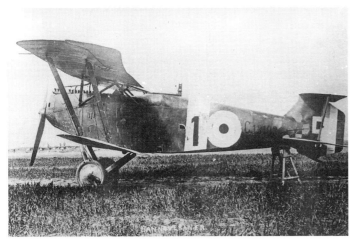

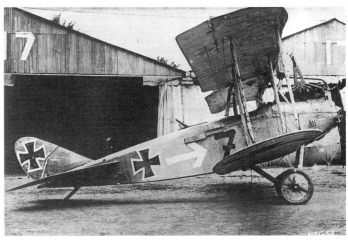

Above left: **Hannover CLII C13103/17 (as a captured aircraft it became G/3 Bgde/2).** (Capt. D.S. Glover)

Above right: **DFW CV. This reconnaissance aircraft was a major success and over 1,000 were produced.** (Capt. D.S. Glover)

Left: **RFC examination of a DFW CV.** (Ken Delve Collection)

Right: **A Nieuport 17 in German hands.** (IWM Q68969)

Above: **Friedrichshafen FF33I;** this was the final version of the excellent FF series of seaplanes. With its Benz BzIII engine it had an endurance of almost six hours. (Peter Green Collection)

Right: The German armed raider Wolf carried a Friedrichshafen seaplane and this played a vital role in the activities of the ship, from reconnaissance for likely victims to bombing. (IWM Q23869)

Below: **La Lovie airfield, Belgium 1917.** (Ken Delve Collection)

Above, centre and below: **Sequence of three photographs showing the 21 Squadron Sports Day at La Lovie in 1917. Other than visits to local hostelries, most entertainment was of such 'home-grown' variety.** (Ken Delve Collection)

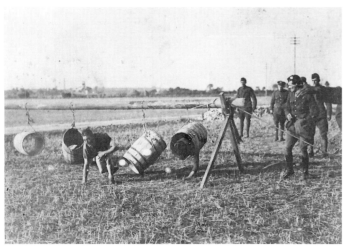

Right: **21 Squadron group at La Lovie October 1917; the Squadron had been at this airfield since March operating RE8s.** (Ken Delve Collection)

Left: **Artillery co-operation was one of the most dangerous of roles; this 21 Squadron RE8 was involved in a shoot over Ypres in October when a 'shell passed through the aircraft'.** (Ken Delve Collection)

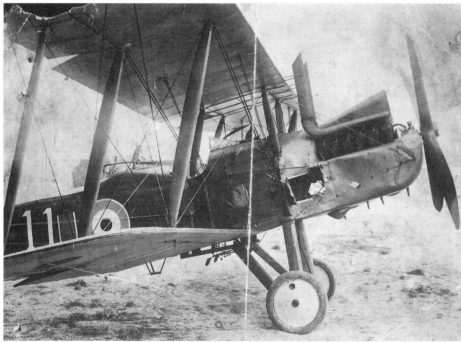

Right: **Sopwith Baby – the type was designed as a scout-bomber to operate from seaplane carriers in the Mediterranean and around the UK. N1452, here, was delivered to Calshot in October.** (Peter Green Collection)

Above: **Very rare shot of a Sopwith Baby firing Le Prieur rockets at the Isle of Grain. Despite doubts (and lack of operational success) with this weapon, a wide range of aircraft were so equipped.** (Peter Green Collection)

Above: **The RFC does not appear to have lost its sense of humour: this was 21 Squadron's Christmas card for 1917.** (Ken Delve Collection)

Below: **The need to get fighters to sea and the slow development of true aircraft carriers, led to a number of ship modifications; here Sopwith Pup N6459 sits on a turret platform aboard HMS *Repulse* in October 1917.** (Peter Green Collection)

Right: **Attaching bombs to the racks beneath an RE8 of 69 Squadron at Savy, October 1917. The unit subsequently became 3 Squadron AFC at Bailleul.** (Ken Delve Collection)

Left: **An RE8 of 3 Squadron AFC about to start for another night bombing mission.** (Ken Delve Collection)

Below: **An RE8 of 3 Squadron AC at Bailleul, 30 November 1917. Note the Presentation Aircraft inscription on the fuselage of A3662.** (Ken Delve Collection)

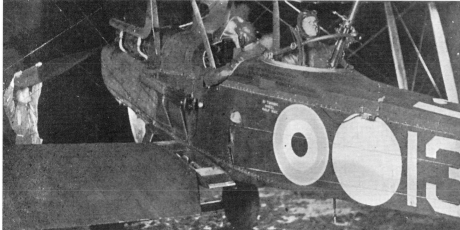

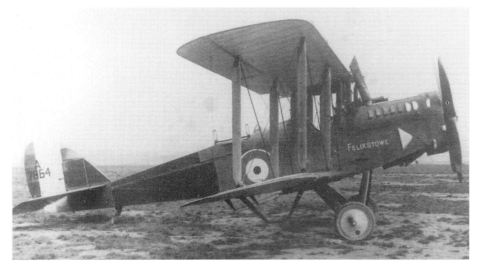

Left: The RFC intensified its bombing campaign during 1917 with a variety of types taking part, such as this 55 Squadron DH4. The squadron had, in January, been the first DH4 unit and had moved to France in March. (Ken Delve Collection)

Right: The aircraft salvage depot at St Omer repaired or cannibalized many aircraft. Seen here are two 57 Squadron DH4s whilst in the background are SE5a's and a Camel. (Ken Delve Collection)

Left: Former 57 Squadron DH4s being used to teach prop swinging. (Ken Delve Collection)

Above left: **The new DH9 day bomber was well into its testing period by autumn 1917 and despite a number of problems was put into large-scale production, reaching operational service in the spring of 1918.** (Ken Delve Collection)

Above right: **Good view of the DH9 front cockpit, with Capt. D.S. Glover in C6117. Armament was usually a single Vickers and single Lewis plus up to four 112lb (50kg) bombs.** (Capt. D.S. Glover)

Right: **DH9 D1651 was one of a batch built by Mann Egerton.** (Ken Delve Collection)

Left: **Line of 84 Squadron SE5as, probably late 1917.** (Ken Delve Collection)

Below: **The Sopwith Pup was gradually replaced in the latter part of 1917, 54 Squadron being one of the last units.** (Ken Delve Collection)

Left: 65 Squadron pilots with one of their Sopwith Camels; the Squadron had acquired Camels in October as they departed for France. (Ken Delve Collection)

Right: With their Squadron markings prominent on the fuselage these are Camels of 45 Squadron. B5152 was with the Squadron for a few weeks from early October 1917 but was shot down on 26 October, 2nd Lt. E. Smith being taken prisoner. In some records B3925 does not appear as having served with the unit – although this photograph is fairly unequivocal. (Ken Delve Collection)

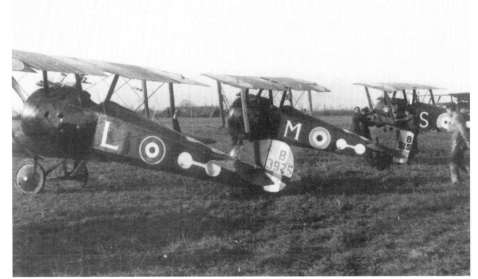

Above: The RNAS and RFC made great use of the Camel from mid 1917 to the end of the war. B6299 served with 10 Squadron RNAS in late 1917 and scored a number of victories; it subsequently returned to the UK to join 207 Training Depot Station at Chingford. (Harry Holmes)

Right: The most significant event on the Eastern Front was the Bolshevik revolution in Russia that led to the Russian exit from the war. This Nieuport 17 was in Russian service and, as shown by the markings, went on to serve the Bolshevik forces. (MAP)

Right: By 1917 the Italians had an increasing number of their own designs entering service; such as this SIA 7B reconnaissance aircraft from Società Italiana Aviazione, a subsidiary of FIAT. The type developed structural problems and was withdrawn in July 1918. This aircraft, '5870, was photographed at Lympne having flown from Turin to Hounslow on a liaison visit. (Capt. D.S. Glover)

Left: The Ansaldo SVA. The SVA series of reconnaissance aircraft were among the best of the war, from the SVA 4 and SVA 5 of 1917 through to the two-seat SVA 9 and SVA 10. This aircraft is seen at Hounslow. (Capt. D.S. Glover)

Right: The Maachi-built Nieuport 11, of which almost 650 were built under licence, was a standard fighter with the Italians up to the summer of 1917. (Ken Wixey Collection)

127

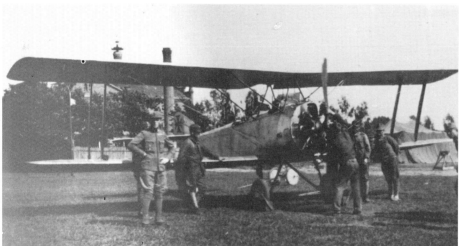

Above: **Brandenburg DI in Austrian service.** (Grosz)

Left: **Other Allied types were also in use over the Italian Front – this Sopwith 1½ Strutter was captured by the Austrians and is here being prepared for a flight.** (Peter Green Collection)

Left: **Phönix-built Hansa-Brandenburg DI of Fliegerkompanie 24 at Pergrine in summer 1917.** (*FlyPast* Collection)

Left: **Frank Linke-Crawford alongside his Albatros DIII serving with Fliegerkompanie 41J at Sesana, October 1917. This Austrian ace scored 27 confirmed victories before being killed in action on 31 July 1918.** (D'Ami)

Right: **Isonzo Front with two Aviatik DIs and two KD fighters at Divacca.** (Meindl)

Below: **The battles around the Isonzo were fierce both on the ground and in the air; a line-up of Hansa-Brandenburg CIs of Fliegerkompanie 101G at Ivacca, late 1917.** (Meindl)

Left: **Phönix-built Hansa-Brandenburg CI of Fliegerkompanie 35 being loaded with bombs; this unit formed in November 1916 and spent its first year on the Isonzo Front.** (Grosz)

Right: **Lohner flying-boat of the Austrian Navy. Although never strong in numbers, the Austrian naval aviators dominated air operations in the Adriatic.** (IWM Q68845)

Left: **Aviatik CI. Note the Schwarztuze machine gun fitted by the Austrian units.** (IWM Q69463)

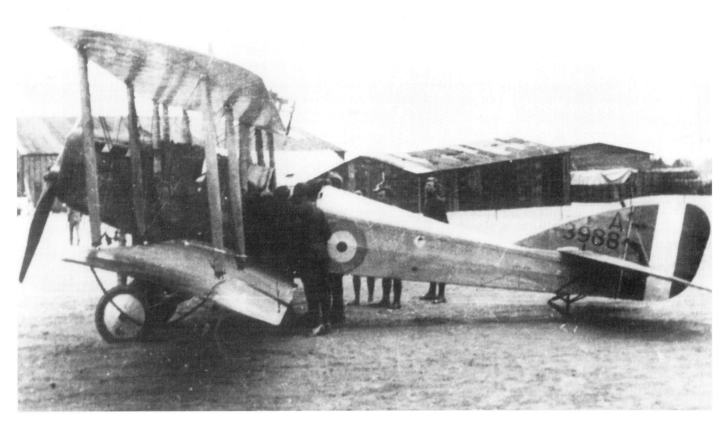

Above: **Martinsyde 'Elephant' A3988 at Salonica, possibly a 14 Squadron machine; the Squadron had been operating in the Middle East since November 1915, with detachments in Palestine, the Western Desert and Arabia.** (Peter Green Collection)

Below: **17 Squadron crews relax at Mikra Bay, Salonica – a base they occupied from July 1916 to September 1918 while operating against the Turkish forces on the Macedonian Front.** (Ken Delve Collection)

Above: **Maj. J.H. Heming of 17 Squadron at Mikra Bay after his flight over and around Mount Olympus.** (Ken Delve Collection)

Left: **Mikra Bay, Salonica 1917 – home to 16 Wing RFC, including 17 Squadron.** (Ken Delve Collection)

Above: **One of three M-series designs from Bristol, the M1C was the only one to see real operational service – primarily in the Middle East and Macedonia. In Palestine 111 Squadron had three M1Bs on strength. This particular M1C was in use with the CFS.** (Peter Green Collection)

Right: **The Turkish Navy operated a number of Gotha WD12 seaplanes; its duration of over five hours made it useful for patrols over the Black Sea.** (MAP)

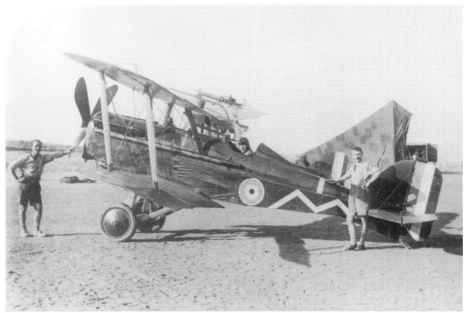

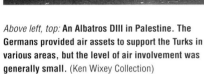

Above left, top: **An Albatros DIII in Palestine. The Germans provided air assets to support the Turks in various areas, but the level of air involvement was generally small.** (Ken Wixey Collection)

Above left, bottom: **Albatros DVa in Palestine; note the tropical kit worn by the ground crew.** (Ken Wixey Collection)

Above right: **111 Squadron also used the SE5a, as with C1764 here. The Squadron had formed at Deir-el-Belah in August 1917 as a fighter unit to support the planned autumn offensive. The SE5a was first used from October.** (IWM Q69445)

Right: **The BE2 series, as with this BE2e, soldiered on in the Middle East, this particular example being the first BE2e actually constructed in Egypt.** (Peter Green Collection)

Below: **From October 1917, 63 Squadron operated the RE8 from Basra and various detachments at other airfields.** (Andy Thomas Collection)

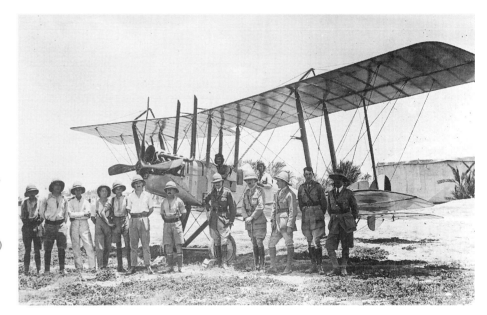

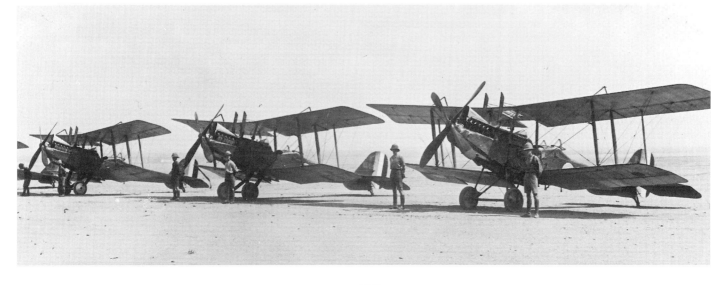

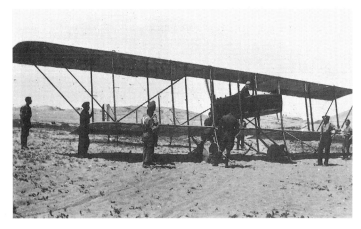

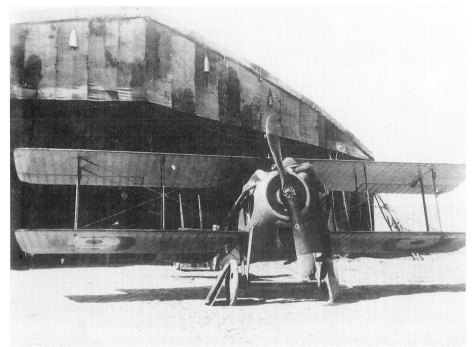

Above left: Egypt was the main location for the various training schools within the Middle East; this Maurice-Farman was with the School of Aerial Gunnery – until written off when a BE2c landed on it! (Ken Delve Collection)

Above right: **Spring 1917 view of an airfield 'in the Suez area'. From having had almost no air assets in 1914, the Middle East strength was appreciable, although spread over a wide area, by late 1917.** (Ken Delve Collection)

Left: **More advanced types were also present – such as this Spad VII.** (Ken Delve Collection)

Right: **BE2e '1808 and '4138 outside a hangar at an airfield in Egypt.** (Ken Delve Collection)

CHAPTER FOUR

1918

The RFC had a good selection of effective types by January 1918 and production of aircraft was more than keeping up with loss rates. Likewise, the training organization was providing a steady stream of new aircrew. The German aircraft industry was being asked to produce 2,000 aircraft and 2,500 aero engines per month but production problems continued to keep deliveries below the planned levels. The German air arm had entered a period when its resources would be in decline, and at an increasing rate. However, a determined effort was made to find qualitative superiority in the absence of numerical parity.

February saw 23 aircraft types entered for the fighter aircraft competition held at Berlin–Adlershof; all but three were biplane designs using proven and reliable engines. The main test was a comparative one of climb performance and testing was carried out by front line pilots. The winner was the Albatros DVa with a high-compression 185hp BMW IIIa engine but best overall was the Fokker VII and this, after certain modifications, entered production as the Fokker DVII with an initial order for 400 aircraft. However, as some of the fighter designs were not quite ready for the February test it was decided to hold a second session in May and this time some 37 designs were tested – no less than ten coming from Fokker – among which was the almost futuristic all-metal low-wing cantilever Ju 9 (D-1) monoplane.

The overall winner of the May test was the Fokker DVII. This aircraft was destined to be one of the outstanding fighters of the war: it had a good overall performance, especially manoeuvrability, plus a pair of reliable and effective Spandau machine guns. Despite its agility it was also easy to fly – a feature lacking in many other fighters of this period. Indeed, it has been said that the DVII had the ability to make a mediocre pilot into a good pilot.

Typical of the combat reports for the Fokker DVII was this by Friedrich Altemeier of Jasta 24 for 24 February 1918:

At 1.35 I started . . . on an orientation flight. At the front we came across four RE8s who immediately turned and tried to flee . . . when the enemy had reached our line, I quickly turned around and attacked one at 88m height SW of St Quentin. Because the enemy was very slow I was able to push the machine down towards Origny behind our lines. Coming very close I fired 50 shots. I had to veer off to avoid a collision with an Albatros . . . I then attacked the RE8 again. I fired another 200 rounds from a very short range. During this attack, several shots were put into my aircraft by the very good shooting of the observer. I attacked again, saw the observer collapse and not shoot anymore, whereas the pilot went down in a very unsteady glide flight and landed. [Friedrich Altemeier, *Cross & Cockade International*]

Altemeier had to make a forced landing because his engine had been damaged.

The early part of the year saw the French create combined operations wings, bringing together fighters and bombers under the same command; typical of this move was the creation of Groupement Ménard, comprising No. 1 Combat Wing, with three groups each of four Spad squadrons, and No. 17 Bomber Wing, with three groups each of three Breguet day bomber squadrons. Groupement Ménard comprised GC15, GC18 and GC 19 and was formed on 4 February; it was followed on 21 February by Groupement Féquant with GC 11, GC 13 and GC 17. One of the Spad squadrons with GC 15 was the famous SPA 81 Escadrille des Lévriers (Greyhound Squadron) and in early 1918 they were cited in a IInd Army Order as an 'élite unit whose pilots enspirited by the example of their chief, Capitaine Bailly, vied among themselves in skill and courage. Although only recently formed, it has remarkable efficiency, asserts its superiority over the enemy and obtains control each time it takes to the air. In eight months it has downed 26 enemy aircraft.' These new groups were mobile, the idea being for them to move to those areas of the front where they were most needed.

The creation of the Royal Air Force on 1 April 1918 was a momentous occasion although in the midst of the continuing fierce conflict on the Western Front it could not, and did not, disrupt the operational efficiency of the RFC or RNAS, which were now joined in the new independent air arm. The only immediate change was in the numbering of RNAS units, achieved by adding 200 to their designation. Thus No. 1 squadron RNAS became No. 201 Squadron RAF.

Submarine War

As this last year of the war opened, the U-boat threat to Allied shipping was still causing concern, though with a greater number of aircraft now flying anti-submarine patrols the U-boats were finding their task increasingly difficult. In January there were 314 aircraft, of which 291 were seaplanes, active in British home waters on anti-submarine work and this number rose gradually throughout the year, reaching 557 by November – somewhat short of the almost 1,200 that had been envisaged. The greatest increase was in the number of land-based and carrier aircraft, even though some of these, like the DH6, were of limited use because of their inability to carry large bombs. However, in April 1918 one of the most effective of such aircraft entered service – the Blackburn Kangaroo.

This was also the year in which the Royal Navy at last brought its aircraft carriers into service. Rear-Admiral R.H. Phillimore – newly appointed to the post of Admiral Commanding Aircraft, established in January – transferred his flag to

HMS *Furious* in March. This carrier was equipped with Sopwith Camels and 1½ Strutters. The carrier was soon engaged on sweeps of the North Sea with the cruiser force, as well as carrying out a number of special operations, usually connected with bombing attacks on enemy installations – such as that on 19 July against the naval airship sheds at Tondern. Capt. B.A. Smart led a number of Camels to attack the sheds and they claimed the destruction of L-54 and L-60.

There was also a requirement to counter the aggressive operations of the German seaplane fighters that had continued to plague the British anti-submarine patrols – two Large America flying boats had been shot down in the first half of the year. The seaplanes were also being used in connection with the extensive German minefields, to guide submarines through cleared channels and to hamper Allied reconnaissance. They were not adverse to attacking surface vessels, and on 11 August a force of six motor boats had been attacked by twelve German seaplanes. All six motor boats were lost: 'the German seaplanes must thus be credited with having made the most successful air operation against light surface craft throughout the war.' Various attempts were made to attack the home bases of these units but none was successful.

Spring Offensive

The Allies had been conducting an intensive bombing campaign since February, with German aerodromes being a prime target. However, on 9 April it was the Germans who launched their attack. In what was to become known as the Battle of the Lys they attacked the British around Hazebrouck.

Preparations had been thorough and the arrival of new units had been kept secret:

It was imperative for the purposes of secrecy that the enemy reconnaissance machines should be kept away from the region through which we proposed to advance. Scouts were therefore patrolling those sectors in order to chase off hostile aeroplanes that attempted to break through. Newly arrived squadrons were not allowed to fly over the lines lest the enemy should learn of our concentration through an increase in the casualties. [P. Neumann, *The German Air Force in the Great War*]

As the Germans advanced, the RAF threw most of its units into helping the ground battle and there was no shortage of targets with troop columns, batteries and ammunition wagons moving in the open. The flyers were 'inspired with the consciousness that they were directly helping to stem the enemy advance.' Contact patrols were equally important in the confused battlefield although these and other roles such as artillery co-operation proved difficult due to disruption of communications as positions rapidly changed – a situation that the German air units found equally frustrating.

Likewise, the German attack units were active; Oscar Bechtle was commanding Schlachstaffel 2 during this period:

assigned in support of assault troops we could be as effective a destructive force as the cavalry had been in the past . . . An hour before daybreak on March 21 the aeroplanes were ready for take-off with two or three 12½kg bombs, in addition to hand-grenades and machine gun ammunition, were loaded into each Halberstadt . . . At last at about 1500 hours the message came – 'support the infantry attack on the Holnon Woods' – less than 10 minutes later we were in the air.

When the patrol arrived over St Quentin,

everywhere beneath us columns were moving west . . . we roared down over our old positions and received signals from our troops there . . . once more we circled and then, in line with our artillery fire, we advanced on the enemy. The pilots opened up with their forward machine-guns, pouring tracer and regular bullets into the enemy positions. Now at last we were there. We passed over the British defences quicker than we thought we would. Down went our hand-grenades, followed by black smoke rising from the ammunitions stockpiles that we had ignited.

The British were soon pushed back over the Somme and in desperate fighting the presence of air support often prevented total collapse. The Germans dominated the air in those areas in which they elected to do so while the Allied bomber squadrons, despite heavy losses, had a vital role to play in disrupting German follow-on forces. By late March the situation had begun to stabilize as British air and ground reinforcements arrived. Almost all air effort was thrown into the ground war; 28 March saw the Allies back at what was known as the Amiens Defence Line – and there they held.

The critical day was 12 April and the RAF flew the most intensive air operations of the war so far, the presence of the aircraft doing much to boost the morale of the hard-pressed infantry. It was also a day of heavy air combat and the RAF claimed 49 enemy aircraft destroyed, six of which fell to Capt. H. Woollett of 43 Squadron during two sorties. His sixth victim was recorded as follows: 'On returning over the lines, I climbed up and found another enemy aeroplane at about 2,000 ft; this after about 20 rounds, collapsed in the air and fell to bits.'

It was during this series of air battles that the famous Red Baron fell. On 21 April Richthofen was leading JG1 to combat a British patrol in the Villiers–Bretonneux area. They were engaged by Camels of 209 Squadron and Capt. R.A. Brown chased the red Triplane down to low level where it crashed. Richthofen had been killed by a single bullet wound to the chest, but it is not clear who caused the fatal wound – Brown or the infantry who opened fire on the Triplane.

By this time the French had already implemented a change of air doctrine, Pétain having ordered the formation of day and night bomber wings, the intention being to wield massed aviation power: 'with bombs and machine guns our planes will set upon columns in march, convoys, bivouacs, and parks, day and night . . . the concentration of aeronautical means necessary to demoralise troops destined to lead and feed the attack.'

Between mid March and mid June French units were in almost constant action over the enemy positions enforcing this doctrine; during this period they dropped over 1,200 tons of bombs. Fighter aviation was also committed to the land battle, to strafe enemy troops and to avoid air combat. In April Group Féquant joined with Group Ménard to form a combat operational group known as Division Aérienne under the command of Gen. Duval. This was in due course further modified to assume a purely tactical role with the fighter element being replaced by heavily armed and armoured types more suited to the close air support role.

The bomber units were equipped with the excellent Breguet 14 B2 and in addition to the protection from the roving Spads they had immediate cover provided by the 'protection squadrons' of Caudron R11s. These latter carried five machine guns, manned by well-trained gunners.

By May the excellent Fokker DVII was appearing at the front in appreciable numbers but although they had an increasing impact on the air war it was too late for them to have a decisive effect; the tide of the war was turning against the Germans. Nevertheless, Ludendorff continued his offensive strategy with a new attack against the French on the Aisne, launching this on 27 May and following it with an attack at Noyon–Montdidier in early June. Both were supported by large formations of aircraft, up to 40 fighters acting in concert. Once again additional fighter strength had been moved in secret to the area to guarantee local air superiority in the area of the attack.

To bolster the French units, British aircraft provided support in the Beauvois sector. The Germans, meanwhile, had thrown almost their entire bomber force into supporting the battlefield, especially with night raids against rear areas, the principal targets being ammunition dumps. Such raids led to the deployment of 151 Squadron, a specialist night fighter unit equipped with Camels, and the unit was soon proving its worth by taking heavy toll of the raiders.

One of the most successful of German aircraft at the time was the Rumpler CVII in its high-level reconnaissance role. Its performance was good enough to keep it out of the range of most Allied fighters and so the German commanders were still able to obtain vital reconnaissance information despite an ever-worsening air situation. The other problem for the Germans from May onwards was a shortage of aviation fuel and this led to a reduction in the level of operational flying – a situation that was to recur in the later stages of the Second World War and one that on both occasions had a significant impact on the air war. The Germans knew that they would never again achieve anything like parity of numbers in the air and so concentrated their effort on achieving technical superiority. This was very much the basis of the strategic plans that were being made in the spring of 1918.

The air war was often a game of cat and mouse, as exemplified by an incident on 5 June:

> Lt E C Bromley and 2nd Lt C G Gass, while leading a patrol of 22 Squadron, sighted a Halberstadt two-seater which on their approach fired a green light. Lt Bromley, suspecting a trap, waited, and in a short time some Albatros scouts appeared and joined the Halberstadt. Almost at once, six Albatros scouts dived out of the sun on the others, apparently mistaking them for one of our patrols. Lt Bromley then led the patrol into the mêlée and shot down the Halberstadt.

Although the first operational American unit, the 103rd, had been operational with the French 4th Army since February, it was spring before any significant new units joined the war. The first operational missions by American Air Service unit thus took place in April; the 94th Pursuit Squadron had flown its first sorties on 14 April – a number of aircraft were out on patrol when news was received of enemy aircraft, two fighters were scrambled from their base and the pilots, Lt. Douglas Campbell and Lt. Alan Winslow, shot down two enemy aircraft (an Albatros DVa and Pfalz DIIIa of Jasta 64).

The first artillery observation unit, the 91st Aero Squadron, flew its first operational mission on 6 June in the Toul sector, which was 'chosen as the place where American squadrons would be located and given their final practice to bridge the gap which must always exist between training schools and work under actual war conditions.' This was to be a quiet part of the front until later in the year and the St Mihiel offensive. The First Corps Observation Group, of three squadrons, had been formed in April and under the tactical control of the French 37th Army had worked with French squadrons, indeed most of the observers in this unit had served with French squadrons. The first day bomber unit, 96th Aero Squadron, flew its first mission on 12 June with an attack by six aircraft on the Dommary–Baroncourt rail yards. This unit was equipped with Breguet 14 B2s, all of which were former instructional aircraft and therefore not in particularly good condition.

Expansion was quite rapid and by May the First Pursuit Group – of four squadrons – had been formed, gaining valuable experience from the pilots of the old Escadrille Américaine.

Among the American pilots establishing a reputation as air fighters was Eddie Rickenbacker. His combat report of 5 June read:

> met a biplane Rumpler over Void, flying at 6000m. Attacked him over Vaulcouleurs after gaining equal height, but was unable to do anything but harass him owing to lack of being able to manoeuvre with him. The fight continued until over Commercy when both my guns had jams which I was unable to fix in the air. However, I continued to manoeuvre as though attacking him, until about 6 miles north of St Mihiel when my motor stopped owing to defective bearings. Started gliding and landed at Menil-la-Tour.

The need for air power was so great that even fairly inexperienced units were soon being moved to more active parts of the front; in July the First Corps Observation Group, under Billy Mitchell, was moved to the Marne sector to work with Gen. Pershing's First Army. A minor British attack, by Australian and American divisions, captured the Villers–Bretonneux plateau on 4 July in preparation for the next major offensive. It made good use of air support and 'fired a large number of rounds and dropped a great many bombs on hostile batteries and troops from a low height.' Aircraft were also used to drop ammunition to the advancing troops. However, 15 July saw the Germans try their last stroke with an attack on French positions around Reims (the fourth Battle of the Champagne). Although the land battle only involved French, American and Italian troops, they were supported by almost 200 aircraft of the RAF's IXth Brigade in addition to their own aircraft.

Three days later, on 18 July, Foch launched his counter-offensive, which effectively halted the German advance – they were never to move forward again. A complex air support plan had been devised for this offensive with a crucial role for the Aerial Division in attacking enemy positions and providing fire support for advancing French troops. Foch also had under his direct control a special unit of three Breguet squadrons, Weiller Group, and these undertook daily reconnaissance of the area 20 to 100km behind the enemy lines. The photographs these aircraft brought back were then used to choose the best targets for the offensive aircraft to attack; the majority of French bomber effort was expended in battlefield support and other than a few night operations there was almost no strategic offensive – even though in May Pétain had included just such a bomber in his plans in order to 'paralyse the economic life of Germany and its war industry by the methodical, massive and repeated action against the principal industrial cities, important marshalling yards, and to weaken the morale of its population by giving them a feeling of insecurity.'

The war-winning Allied offensive was opened on 8 August in the Amiens area by Rawlinson's 4th Army. Air support was both detailed and well integrated: 'pilots were to try to obtain as much information as possible about the ground situation, and squadron commanders were to ensure that this information reached the proper quarters using the pre-arranged scheme.' Each of the squadrons was to send aircraft in pairs at 30 minute intervals in order to provide continuous air cover, each to be armed with four 25lb (11kg) bombs. Before long I, III and IX Brigades had joined V Brigade and RAF aircraft were heavily engaged in attacking the enemy wherever possible in the air and on the ground. Airfields, bridges over the Somme and a host of other targets came under attack. The low-flying bombers began to suffer from German fighter attention and so fighter escort was provided for many of the missions. Shortage of aircraft, pilots, supplies and fuel were having a devastating effect on the German air arm as was the almost continual retreat; all available aircraft, including the night bombers, were thrown into the battle in a futile effort to prevent total defeat.

From time to time they managed to achieve a local superiority by concentrating upwards of 60 aircraft at one point, such as the defence of the Somme bridges when in a four-day period the Allies failed to destroy the bridges and the Germans claimed 144 aircraft shot down for the loss of 30 of their own – but whereas the Allies could stand the loss, the Germans could not. July had seen the RAF lose two of its greatest air fighters – James McCudden being killed in a flying accident on 9 July and Mick Mannock falling on 26 July to ground fire.

German naval aviation was in somewhat better shape and was able to remain rather more effective during 1918 despite a shortage of aircraft; types such as the Hansa-Brandenburg W.29 maintained the technical superiority. Fritz Stormer served with such a unit:

> opposing the enemy seaplane units in our area was comparatively easy to do as our Hansa-Brandenburg monoplanes were superior to the British flying-boats in terms of speed, manoeuvrability and armament . . . we did more than just interdict enemy aircraft; indeed, our main mission was devoted to the surveillance of maritime traffic in the entire blockade sector from the English coast to Holland. [Fritz Stormer, *Cross & Cockade International*, Vol. 20/2]

Kite balloons were still an important reconnaissance medium for the ground forces and the Allies paid a great deal of attention to destroying them. They were considered of such value that, of course, the enemy tried their best to protect them through the use of anti-aircraft positions and even their own fighter cover. The RAF developed special tactics to ensure success: 'the lead flight was made up of four or five experienced pilots who could be trusted to shoot straight and fend for themselves. This was the striking force. The other two flights acted as cover. The force crossed the lines at 10,000ft as if on an offensive patrol, 'A' Flight would then dive on the balloons while the others provided cover.' [AP125]

A number of squadrons, such as 84 Squadron, began to specialize in this role and on one day this unit accounted for seven balloons. Furthermore, one of its pilots, Capt. A.W. Beauchamp-Proctor, claimed 16 balloons over a period of 18 months – the Squadron total being 50 for the same period. Capt. H.W. Woollett of 43 Squadron

> attacked a hostile balloon and fired about 60 rounds into it; the two observers jumped out and the balloon fell in flames. He then attacked another hostile balloon which went down in flames, no-one was seen to jump out of this balloon. A few minutes later Capt. Woollett attacked a third balloon which was being pulled down, but after he had fired about 50 rounds into it the hostile balloon fell in flames. [AP125]

Another of the great 'balloon busters' was Frank Luke. His operational period lasted only a few weeks in August and September but during that time he scored 21 victories, his speciality being the destruction of balloons. It was on one such unauthorized sortie that he was shot down; having destroyed three balloons his badly damaged aircraft crashed and he then chose to fire his revolver at the approaching German infantry and so was shot dead.

The increasing use of tanks, and other changes in ground force tactics, led to specialization by RAF units and closer co-operation, including training, with ground units; typical of this was the allocation in the summer of 8 and 73 Squadrons for co-operation with the Tank Corps. The entire air war scenario was becoming more complex, integrated and co-ordinated. As part of the plan to win total air supremacy, Allied fighter sweeps would force the enemy to scuttle back to their aerodromes – which were then promptly attacked by bombers and fighters.

Typical of the airfield attacks at this period was that of 13 August against Varssenaere in the northern sector; 50 Camels from Dunkirk and a number of DH9s made a dawn attack on this important airfield. A great deal of detailed planning had gone into the attack and it was a superb success. When they arrived there were three flights of Fokkers lined up ready to go:

> for the next 10 minutes or so the scene was one of indescribable chaos; sheds and huts burning, aircraft on the ground wrecked and in flames, while, over the whole, hung clouds of thick grey smoke through which British and American aircraft [the latter being 17 Aero Squadron] dived and wheeled, firing streams of machine-gun bullets into the various targets.

Another such raid was against Haubourdin by four squadrons, 65 aircraft, of 80 Wing led by Lt.-Col. L.A. Strange a few days later:

> This impressive air fleet, loaded with incendiary and explosive bombs and all the machine-gun ammunition it could carry, gained its height over Reclinghem aerodrome at 1230 p.m. . . . The plan was for the two layers of the fleet to attack the objective in turn while the Bristol Fighters and the British SE5s ensured protection from possible attack . . . As the first flight dived upon the westernmost hangars of the aerodrome, a Fokker biplane, which was caught in the air at the time, flew straight into a tree. In all 136 25lb and six 40lb bombs were dropped and a large number of rounds fired from 400ft to 50ft. Three large hangars containing aircraft were completely burnt, and two aeroplanes standing outside were set on fire. Several other hangars received direct hits and considerable casualties were caused amongst personnel of the aerodrome.

It was a far cry from the days in 1914 and 1915 when an appearance over an enemy aerodrome usually signalled the dropping of a message. While the land battle went into a pause on 11 August, the air campaign continued to prepare the way for the next push. There had been errors in the use of air power during the Amiens offensive but the RAF had now established its overall dominance.

The first significant American offensive took place in September at St Mihiel and each of the Army Corps was given an air observation Group. The overall air strength was boosted by the presence of British units, including the Independent Force, and French units. The offensive was launched on 12 September and it went well from the start:

> the enemy pursuit fought tenaciously in an effort to cover the German retreat, but they were heavily outnumbered and succeeded only rarely

in approaching the line of battle to attack any observation planes. They did, however, inflict heavy casualties upon our day bomber airplanes, French, English and American, when the latter penetrated deep into the enemy rear areas. [*United States Air Service in The First World War*]

The First Day Bombardment Group was also involved in the offensive. Karl Payne was an observer with the 96th Aero Squadron:

September 12, first operations, day one of the St Mihiel push. At this time it was believed that our planes, the Liberty DH4s, could be used as biplane fighters. However, this proved impracticable and the Squadron was assigned to daylight bombing. The morning of September 14 we made our first bombing raid, the first squadron of American-built machines to bomb the enemy. In spite of adverse conditions due to lack of familiarity with the planes and work, the Squadron made eight raids in three days. [Karl Payne, *Cross & Cockade International*, Vol. 21/4]

Strategic Bombing

The most significant event as regards the Allied strategic bombing offensive was the formation, on 6 June, of the RAF's Independent Force. This organization had its origins in October 1917 with the formation of 41 Wing RFC, which at first comprised only three squadrons – 100 Squadron with the FE2b, 55 Squadron with the DH4 and 16 (Naval) Squadron with Handley Page bombers. The unit's headquarters was at Bainville-sur-Madon and it was commanded by Lt.-Col. Cyril Newall with the aim of launching a concerted attack against German industrial targets.

By February 1918 the organization had become VIII Brigade and soon added two additional DH9-equipped squadrons. In the period up to June 1918 it carried out 142 raids, 57 of which were to targets in Germany (including Cologne, Stuttgart Mannheim, Mainz and Coblenz). On 6 June Trenchard took command and a further five squadrons were added to give the new organization a formidable day and night capability. Attacks were pressed home with great determination and losses on the daylight missions were often heavy.

On 31 July when 12 DH9s of 99 Squadron were tasked to attack Mainz three of the aircraft turned back early with engine problems (a regular event with the DH9 at

this time) while the rest were shortly afterwards intercepted by 40 enemy aircraft. Four were shot down while five managed to drop their bombs on the rail sidings at Saarbrücken, this having been elected by the leader as a secondary target. Three more were shot down on the return journey and the enemy aircraft were driven off only by the arrival of 104 Squadron.

Certain elements of the Independent Force concentrated on specific roles; for example, 100 Squadron specialized in attacks on German airfields – a particular favourite being Boulay, home of the German night bomber force, while 55 Squadron had extra fuel tanks in their DH4s (to give 5½ hours endurance as against the more usual 3¾ hours) and took on unescorted long-distance day attacks.

Losses remained heavy but the squadrons played a significant role in both a strategic and tactical sense, in the latter case being attached from time to time to co-operate with ground force operations by bombing such targets as rail yards. On 28 November an Air Council memo stated: 'in recent months the work of the Independent Air Force has had moral and material effects which have contributed powerfully to the disintegration of the enemy capacity for resistance.'

The Americans had formed their First Day Bombardment Group, 11th and 20th Squadrons, in September and this unit was soon engaged on a wide range of strategic missions, with rail yards still being high up the list. One of the most useful documents produced by the Americans at the end of the war was the USAS Bombing Survey to assess the effects of the strategic bombing campaign (by all Allied bombers). The survey team visited 140 towns to examine German records. Part of the report for Metz stated: 'Four hours is the average time required to repair tracks when a direct hit is made. The continuous bombing of Metz had a tremendous effect upon the morale of the workers and civilians. They lived almost entirely in their cellars and it was stated that should the bombing have continued a month or so longer, it would have been impossible to keep employees at their duty.'

The report noted that 92 attacks had been made on this target, the first taking place on 10 October 1915 and the last on 10 November 1918 and that 43 of these attacks had been made in 1918. The team also looked at the attacks on industrial targets, typical of these reports being that for the Carl Foundry at Thionville, which

included extracts of German documents such as this one relating the first air raid (16 April 1916):

Four bombs were thrown, the first bomb fell on the oil refiner built in masonry, about 1 sq m of masonry was disturbed. The second fell on the roof of machine house No 2 and exploded on an iron purlin without any significant damage. Bomb three hit the gas connection to machine house No 2; the damage was immediately repaired. Bomb four fell on the roof of the casting house and damaged a great number of roof tiles.

There were numerous follow-on raids and none caused any major physical damage, but the effect on morale was recorded as significant.

The HP 0/400 had entered service with the Independent Force at the end of August, 100 Squadron giving up its FE2bs to become the first to operate this new bomber. Other units likewise re-equipped and the HP became a significant part of the strategic offensive. There were, however, bad nights, the worst being 16/17 September when seven HP 0/400s were lost (including four from 215 Squadron). The following night the German bomber force suffered losses when three of their number were shot down by 151 Squadron.

In early October the 0/400s began to employ the largest bomb used by the RAF: a 1,650lb (750kg) weapon. A special bomber force, 27 Group, was formed in England with 'super Handley Page bombers' – the V/1500 or 'Bloody Paralyser' – in order to bomb Berlin but this unit was not operational before the end of the war.

The German retreat was now almost continuous although there was still heavy fighting on the ground and in the air; reconnaissance became once more of prime importance as Allied commanders tried to discover where to advance and where the Germans were trying to make a stand. In addition, all communications routes – road, rail and water – were kept under continuous attack to add to the chaos, disruption and collapse of German Army morale.

The final great assault on the Hindenburg Line was planned for late September and all aspects underwent detailed preparation and planning; the air involvement was, as usual by this stage of the war, seen as an integrated and vital part of the overall offensive plan. The American First Army instructions to its air elements give an insight into the complex nature of such integration:

1. Pursuit.
   a) The First Pursuit Group (4 Groups) will insure an absolute barrage of the front and protect our observation aviation at every altitude from the Meuse inclusive on the east to La Hazarée inclusive on the west, prevent enemy attack through the Woevre and will attack concentrations of enemy troops, convoys, enemy aviation and balloons.
   b) Pursuit Aviation, French Aerial Division, will be so dispersed as to protect our right flank and front in case of an attack.

2. Day Bomber.
Will attack concentrations of enemy troops, convoys and aviation, railroad stations, command posts and dumps.

3. Night Bomber.
Will attack railroad stations and trains, troop concentrations, ammunition dumps and airdromes.

4. Reconnaissance Aviation.
   a) Army reconnaissance will carry out long-distance missions, both photographic and visual.
   b) Army Corps and Army Artillery will carry out missions, both photographic and visual, prescribed by the Army Corps and Army Artillery commanders including:
      – The observation and results of artillery fire.
      – Liaison with the infantry.
      – Information of the enemy of benefit to the Higher Command.
   c) Night reconnaissance will carry out visual reconnaissance as prescribed.

The night bombing element was provided by one French and one Italian Group; indeed, the air strength under American command included 62 French squadrons in addition to the night bomber group. Nevertheless, the Allied offensive was now unstoppable and at every turn of the battle the air units were closely and intensively engaged. Late September brought the attack on the Hindenburg Line's key positions, although poor weather restricted the air effort in the first few days.

Even as late as October the Fokker DVII was still in a class of its own, although new Allied types that almost matched its performance – such as the Sopwith Snipe – were entering service. The Independent Force continued to take heavy losses and quite

often these fell upon a single squadron on any given day. For example, on 25 September 55 Squadron lost four DH4s, with most of the others damaged, and on the same day 110 Squadron lost six of its DH9As.

Although the war was almost over, the final few days of October saw some of the heaviest air fighting. Large groups of German fighters patrolled key areas; on 30 October the RAF claimed 69 enemy aircraft for 41 of their own lost – the Sopwith Dolphins of 19 Squadron were escorting 98 Squadron's DH9s when they were involved in a fight with large numbers of Fokkers, claiming ten and losing five.

Other Theatres

The problem from German submarines was not confined to British waters, and the Mediterranean was home to a sizeable German U-boat force. To counter this the RNAS and RFC (and later RAF) air elements flew extensive anti-submarine patrols and carried out attacks on their home bases. Carriers, seaplane tenders and shore-based aircraft all took part, as did the kite balloons attached for convoy escort duties.

The Aegean Group's squadrons were dispersed to a number of airfields over the large Salonica operational area and by 1918 had achieved total dominance over their Turkish adversaries and the few German aircraft that still appeared. While Turkish infantry, and to a lesser extent their Bulgarian allies, were some of the most determined of any army they did not cope well with air attacks and morale was at a low ebb. By September the Bulgarian forces were in general retreat and under attack by detachments from the Aegean Group, 'causing considerable damage and dislocation and confusion to the enemy transport and lines of communication; railways, aerodromes, and dumps were also repeatedly bombed to good effect.'

Lines of communication and ports remained high on the target list and throughout the late summer such places as Constantinople, San Giovanni di Medusa, Durazzo (now Durrës) and Rogozina were targeted. Durazzo, for example, was attacked on 2 October in conjunction with operations by the British and Italian fleets. Four waves of escorted bombers attacked the area from 6.15 to 10.50am, dropping bombs on rail sidings and dumps. There were no defending aircraft and anti-aircraft fire was

light. This proved to be the last concentrated air attack on a target on the enemy coast. However, by this time the Bulgarians had already left the war, an armistice having been signed on 29 September.

The Austrians launched a sudden offensive against Italy in the Piave, Montello and Mt Grappa regions in mid June but after early success this had to be abandoned when the Piave flooded, causing total disruption of supply lines. The Italian air strength on this Front stood at 553 aircraft, supported by 20 French and 80 British aircraft. All were heavily engaged on reconnaissance, strafing and bombing, there being little call for major air battles. By now the Pomilio types had replaced the Caudrons with the reconnaissance units and the SIA 7B was the prime artillery co-operations type – despite a continuing problem with this type's tendency to shed its wings in flight!

The RAF's Adriatic Group was attached to the Italian XVI Army Corps for that formation's summer offensive on the Albanian front, the RAF aircraft flying escort for Italian bombers plus a number of airfield attack missions (such as that against Tirana airfield on 6 July). Although air combats were frequent they were pretty much one-sided and RAF aircraft, along with their Italian counterparts, ruled the skies. During July the Allies claimed 72 enemy aircraft destroyed for the loss of only three of their own.

For many months the Italians had desired to visit Vienna from the air and on 9 September this at last took place when eight SVAs flew a 620 mile (1,000km) round-trip to drop leaflets on the Austrian capital. Late October brought the final Italian offensive, culminating in the Battle of Vittorio Veneto on 28 October, which was swiftly followed by the armistice signed on 4 November.

In Palestine the Turkish forces remained strong and the Turkish and German air elements continued to dispute the skies with the RAF units. From April onwards the RAF squadrons carried out a policy of almost daily raids against Turkish positions in order to cause disruption and lower morale. By September, Allenby was ready to launch his final offensive and the RAF commander, Brig.-Gen. A.E. Barton, issued his orders to 'conceal General Allenby's dispositions from the enemy, to destroy his communication centres, and to take an active part in the destruction of his retreating forces.'

The Turkish 7th and 8th Armies were soon in retreat; on 21 September a reconnaissance spotted a large Turkish force on the road leading north-east from Nablus. Every available aircraft was made ready and it was intended to put two over this target every three minutes, with an additional six aircraft every 30 minutes, from 8am to midday. The sides of the road were bordered by steep ravines and so there was no escape after the head of the column had been destroyed, blocking the road: 'never for one moment was there any respite from the pitiless hail of bombs and machine-gun bullets from overhead. By the time the British troops arrived on the scene, the Turkish 7th Army had ceased to exist.' Beirut fell on 8 October and Aleppo on 25 October as the campaign came to an end.

Conclusions

A few hundred unarmed and flimsy aeroplanes had taken to the air in August 1914 and most generals saw only a limited role for these latter-day 'birdmen'. Within a matter of months it was obvious to most that aeroplanes were a vital part of the military art. The call went out for more effective types in greater numbers.

As each year of the war passed so the impact of this third dimension grew. Aircraft bombed cities and industries hundreds of miles from the battlefield, a soldier standing on a railway platform in 'safe' territory suddenly found himself under attack from the enemy, waiting in the rear trenches to join an attack he found the air filled with bombs and machine gun fire. There was no escape from the attentions of the aircraft.

By 1918 the air arms of the major belligerents numbered thousands of aircraft. The 'war to end all wars' had brought air power to prominence; the lessons of this war would affect military planning for the remainder of the twentieth century.

Left: Atmospheric shot of an RE8 at Vert Galand in May 1918; over 2,200 of this type served with the RFC from November 1916 to the end of the war. During this final year of conflict they were still heavily employed but with Allied air superiority, except at certain times, they were able to carry our their work at an 'acceptable' loss rate. (Peter Green Collection)

Below left: **RE8 A4267 with 52 Squadron in early 1918.** (Peter Green Collection)

Below right: **Excellent field hangar shot of ground crew working on an RE8 of 3 Squadron AFC, possibly at Bailleul.** (Ken Delve Collection)

Left: **Unidentified Sopwith Dolphin (possibly C3816) at Beaulieu. As an operational type the aircraft replaced Spads in a number of fighter Squadrons; some were armed with two Vickers plus two Lewis guns giving them a formidable armament.** (Peter Green Collection)

Left: **The Sopwith Dolphin was designed to give the pilot the best possible field of view – hence the low setting of the upper wing – early trials showed great promise in speed and manoeuvrability (the first Martlesham tests having taken place in mid 1917). It was January 1918 before the first fully equipped unit, 19 Squadron, was operational in France. D3775 is seen here with 73 Squadron.** (Peter Green Collection)

Left: **This May 1918 shot shows Dolphin C4172 in service with the School of Special Flying at Gosport.** (Capt. D.S. Glover)

Right: **143 Squadron SE5a D5995 at Throwley; the Squadron operated the type from March to August 1918 when they were replaced by Camels.** (Peter Green Collection)

Right: **Dispersal shot of 6 Squadron AFC with SE5a at Minchampton in spring 1918. All four of the last Australian Squadrons (Nos. 5 to 8) were still working up to operational status during 1918 and did not see active service in France.**

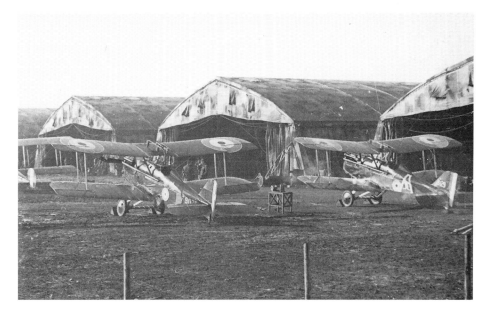

Left: The Sopwith Camel is regarded by many as the finest fighter of the First World War; F6394 was from one of the last Boulton-Paul batches of Camels and was delivered to Martlesham Heath in September 1918. (Ken Delve Collection)

Below: Camel of 66 Squadron. With its good all-round performance and twin Vickers guns, the Camel was a potent fighter in the hands of experienced pilots. (Ken Delve Collection)

Left: 73 Squadron Camel after a mid-air collision on 20 May 1918. The squadron was operating from Beauvois, where they had been since March. (Ken Delve Collection)

Below: Aircrew of 208 Squadron pose with their Camels; the Squadron had formed at Dunkirk from the old 8 Squadron RNAS upon the formation of the Royal Air Force. (Peter Green Collection)

Above: The deleted aircraft serials on this line of 73 Squadron Camels are an attempt to censor the picture. (Ken Delve Collection)

Left: 73 Squadron Camel at Hervilly October 1918, with Lt. Baker, Lt. Reid and Lt. Stieber. (Ken Delve Collection)

Right: Camel B7227 of 10 Squadron RNAS having come to grief behind the German lines after being attacked and shot down on June 21 by four Fokker DVIIs; 2nd Lt. R.G. Carr was taken prisoner. (Harry Holmes)

Above: **In this posed shot crew obey the 'empty your pockets before going on patrol' sign; this was designed to deny useful intelligence to the enemy in the event of the crew ending up behind enemy lines.** (Ken Delve Collection)

Right: **Sopwith Snipe E6274 was one of a batch of 400 produced by Boulton-Paul; it is seen here at Freiston sometime in 1918. Large-scale production orders were issued in March 1918, the type having been selected as a fighter following a Martlesham test earlier in the year.** (Peter Green Collection)

Above: **Bristol Fighter of 11 Squadron; the unit re-equipped with this type in June 1917, giving up its FE2bs.** (Jack Bruce/Stuart Leslie collection)

Left: **73 Squadron crews pose with the 'Squadron Car – a Crossley', in November 1918.** (Ken Delve Collection)

Right: **43 Squadron Snipe with an underfuselage bomb carrier. The Snipe was powered by the 230hp Bentley BR2 and remained in service long after the Armistice.** (Jack Bruce/Stuart Leslie collection)

Left: **32 Squadron arrived in France in May 1916 and spent the rest of the war as a fighter unit, acquiring a distinguished reputation. Here, in early 1918, the crews stand with their SE5a aircraft.** (Ken Delve Collection)

Right: **The sole example of a simplified Albatros fighter, the DIX, was partly an attempt to simplify production at a time when greater numbers of aircraft were required – however, it failed to achieve anything like a reasonable performance and was quite rightly discontinued.** (MAP)

Above: The LFG Roland DVIb was one of the designs for the 1918 fighter competition. The Germans had realized that numerical superiority rested with the Allies and so instead concentrated on trying to achieve technical superiority. Only limited numbers of the Roland VIb were built and they were mainly used by the Navy for seaplane defence duties. (MAP)

Above: Another of the 1918 designs to find little favour was the compact Aviatik DVIII. Although its performance was reasonable it had an endurance of little more than one hour. (MAP)

Left: The Aviatik CIX entered tests in the first part of 1918. Powered by a 200hp Benz IV the aircraft had a top speed of 100mph (160kph) and a ceiling of 14,760ft (4,500m) – quite inadequate for the period. (MAP)

Right: An aircraft of advanced appearance, the Junkers J8 prototype of January 1918 incorporated many new features – not least the all-metal construction. In due course it gave rise to the J10, which subsequently entered production as the CLI. (MAP)

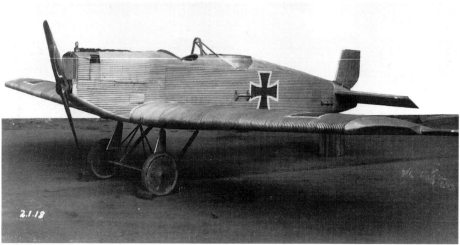

Above: The LVG CVIII was designed for the high-compression 200hp Benz I (to give 240hp) for altitude performance. In the event, however, the prototype was a one-off as production effort was concentrated on more promising types. (MAP)

Above: The Aviatik DIII first appeared in late 1917 but two were entered for the 1918 fighter competition. Despite a reasonable performance it was up against superb designs such as the Fokker DVII and so was abandoned. (MAP)

Below: Albatros DVs and Fokker Triplanes of Jasta 12 line up at Toulis in March 1918. (Ken Delve Collection)

Left: **Outright winner of the fighter competition was the Fokker DVII; the type has been assessed as one of the best three fighters of the war and it certainly caused the Allies many problems during 1918.** (Ken Delve Collection)

Below left: **Emil Thuy was one of a number of German fighter pilots to amass large victory scores. He began his flying career with FFA53 n July 1915 and eventually joined Jasta 21 before moving on to Jasta 28.** (Dennis Hylands)

Above right: **Fokker DVII being inspected by Allied personnel at the end of the war.** (Peter Green Collection)

Left: **Fokker DVIIs of JG3 (Jastas 2 and 36). The nearest aircraft – tail only – is an Albatros DVa.** (Ken Wixey Collection)

Right: **Rear view of the Hannover CLII showing the unusual tail arrangement. This photo is of C131031/17 in May 1918 (a captured aircraft that became G/3Bgde/2).** (Peter Green Collection)

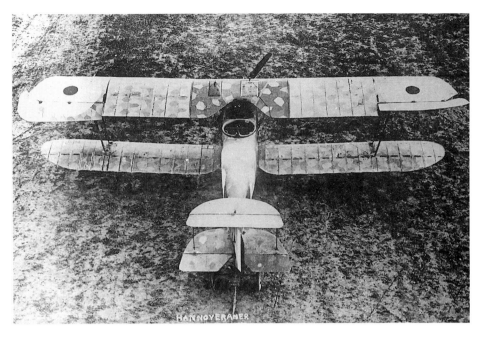

Left: **The Hannover CLIII (or IIIa) was employed on escort fighter and ground support duties, especially the latter. The IIIa was the commonest variant, some 537 being built. Total Hannover CL construction amounted to over 1,000 machines.** (Harry Woodman)

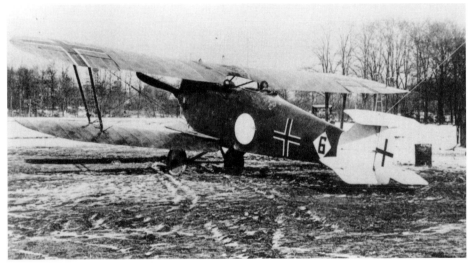

Right: **DFW CV as G/HQ/4.** (Capt. D.S. Glover)

151

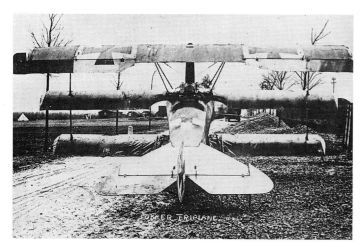

Above left: This Fokker Triplane (probably of Jasta 11) was shot down by anti-aircraft fire on 13 January 1918 and its pilot, Lt. Eberhard Stapenhörst, was taken prisoner. (Capt. D.S. Glover)

Above right: The Albatros CX was still in service during 1918 for reconnaissance and artillery work and continued to be a reliable and effective machine – although vulnerable to the increasing numbers of Allied fighters. (MAP)

Left: Oblt. Ernst Udet with his Fokker DVII. Udet ended the war as the second-highest German scorer with 62 victories and went on to play a significant role in the re-birth of the Luftwaffe in the 1930s. (Ken Delve Collection)

Below: The French fighter units continued to use the Spads and Nieuports to good effect. These Spad VIIs are from SPA97. (IWM Q69540)

Above: **The Breguet 14 A2 reconnaissance aircraft was powered by a 300hp Renault engine; the prototype first flew in November 1918 and the type went into large-scale production.** (Jack Bruce/Stuart Leslie collection)

Right: **'Ace of aces' René Fonck who was credited with 75 victories by the end of the war; his first operational posting had been to Escadrille C47 (flying Caudrons) in June 1915 as a Corporal Pilot.** (Dennis Hylands)

Below: **Nieuport 23 N2903 of N561, a unit that formed part of the air defence of Venice.** (*FlyPast* Collection)

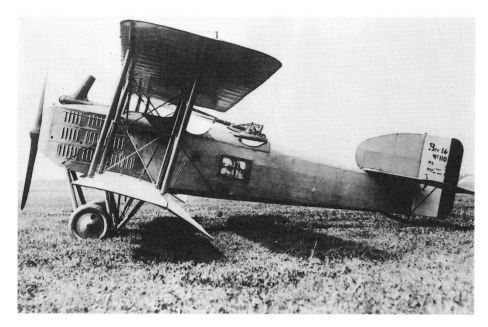

Left: The Breguet 14 B2 prototype was introduced in the French forces in April 1917 as a bigger-winged variant of the successful 14 A2. The bomber variant was given racks under the wings for 32 small-calibre bombs. (Jack Bruce/Stuart Leslie collection)

Below: Breguet 14 A2 reconnaissance machine; over 5,500 Breguet 14s in reconnaissance and bomber variants had been built by the end of the war and production continued into the 1920s. (Ken Wixey Collection)

Below: Aircraft production in Britain was by early 1918 efficient and large numbers of aircraft were being made available from a wide range of companies. Ruston Proctor built well over 1,000 Camels; here D8185 is seen at Monks Road, Lincoln on 1 June 1918 as part of a recruitment procession – the women being known as the 'Ruston Munitionettes'. The first unit for this particular aircraft was 471 Flight at Walmer. (Peter Green Collection)

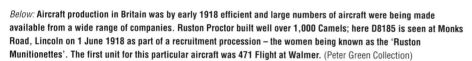

Right: **As well as extensive operational service, the SE5a was used by a number of training units – this particular colourful example is probably an instructor's aircraft.** (Ken Delve Collection)

Left: **SE5a C6414 under construction by Wolseley.** (Peter Green Collection)

Right: **An armed DH6, with a good view of the gun mounting on the upper wing – C7835 at Fowlmere after Sgt. Thompson's 'quarrel with a cottage' in September 1918. Although primarily a training machine, the DH6 was also used for Home Defence and by a number of specialist units such as the School of Aerial Fighting.** (Capt. D.S. Glover)

Right: **1918 and BE2 variants were still in regular use with training units. A1350 of 51 TS is little more than a pile of wood and wire after this crash on 6 January 1918.** (Peter Green Collection)

Above: **Colourful Sopwith Pup B7575 in service with 26 TDS; many instructors' aircraft acquired highly decorative schemes!** (Peter Green Collection)

Above: **The Avro 504 series continued to be the most important of the training machines. This is Avro 504K F2623, one of those built by Sunbeam Motors.** (Harry Holmes)

Left: **The Allied bombing offensive grew in intensity during the summer of 1918. FE2bs continued to act as night bombers; here is a 58 Squadron example – plus a unicycling pilot, possibly W.L. Hope.** (Ken Delve Collection)

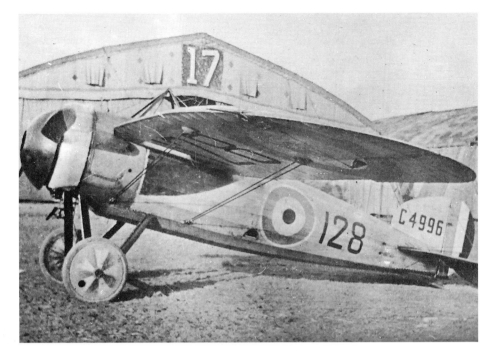

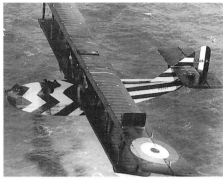

Above right: The Felixstowe flying boats gave valuable service around the shores of the UK in a variety of roles, but primarily on anti-submarine patrols. This aircraft, N4545, arrived at Felixstowe in July 1918 and joined 230 Squadron, which, in August, formed out of the Anti-Submarine Patrol unit. (Peter Green Collection)

Above left: Among the specialist schools that had grown in importance by 1918 was the School of Aerial Warfare. This unit operated a wide range of types, such as this Bristol M1C seen at Marske in 1918. (Peter Green Collection)

Above: The DH9 entered service with 41 Wing in April 1918 (99 and 104 Squadrons) for the strategic bombing offensive; the RAF planned a day and night offensive against targets in Germany but the squadrons were frequently called upon to support the land battle. (*FlyPast* Collection)

Left: Lt. Lawson Reason with DH9 E619 of 98 Squadron; the unit moved to France in April 1918 and flew its first bombing missions on 9 April. (Peter Green Collection)

Above: Its skid-type undercarriage having collapsed, this Pup sits on what is possibly HMS *Argus*. Skid-equipped Pups were certainly aboard HMS *Furious* in early 1918 and by mid year some ten of these aircraft were operational with various carriers. (Peter Green Collection)

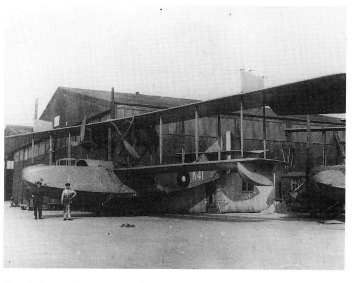

Above: Felixstowe F2A in service with the US Naval Air Service at Killingholme. (Peter Green Collection)

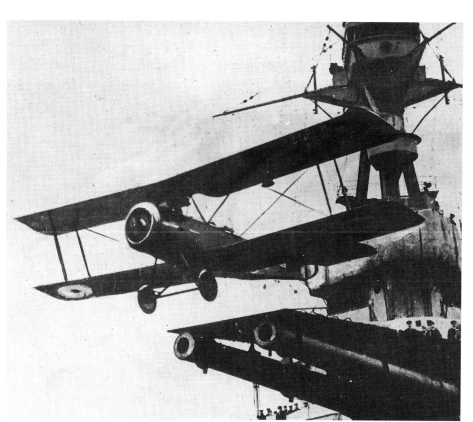

Above: A Sopwith Camel modified with cut-away in the centre section of the upper wing to allow an upward-firing gun to be fitted. This is possibly N6643, one of 50 Sopwith 2F1 'ships Camels' delivered in early 1918. (Harry Holmes)

Left: A Sopwith 1½ Strutter leaving the gun-turret platform of HMS *Barham*. (Capt. D.S. Glover)

Above left: **Prototype Port Grain Griffin, one of a number of designs in 1918 from the Port Victoria design staff and based upon the Sopwith Baby. Only seven production aircraft followed and they saw very little service.** (*FlyPast* Collection)

Above right: **This 73 Squadron photograph, dated June 1918 at Planques, shows Capt. Graham and Capt. Lullier and is entitled 'the first to don the RAF uniform'. The creation of the Royal Air Force on 1 April 1918 was a significant step in the development of British air power, though it had little direct effect on the conduct of the latter part of the First World War.** (Ken Delve Collection)

Above: **Despite the early success of an air-launched torpedo, development of this capability was slow; the Sopwith Cuckoo was designed for the role but did not make an appearance until 1918. This particular aircraft, N6971, was a Blackburn-built example that entered service in August 1918, going to 201 TDS at East Fortune.** (Capt. D.S. Glover)

Right: **Capt. W.E. Johns, author of the *Biggles* novels, in front of an RE8. He was shot down in DH4 F5712 of 55 Squadron on 16 September 1918.** (*FlyPast* Collection)

Above: **Beauvois, 4 September 1918.** (Ken Delve Collection)

Above: **49 Squadron at Vilers-les-Cagincourt in November 1918.** (Ken Delve Collection)

Above: **Beauvois, 26 September 1918** (Ken Delve Collection)

Above: **Bazeul, 24 September 1918.** (Ken Delve Collection)

Above: **2 Squadron shot of Genech, summer 1918.** (Ken Delve Collection)

Above: **Beauvois, 5 July 1918.** (Ken Delve Collection)

Above: The shortage of aircraft for the growing USAS in France led to the purchase of British and French types, including a batch of fifty SE5a fighters – including F8083 shown here. (Peter Green Collection)

Above: Although the United States entered the war in April 1917, it was spring 1918 before any significant number of air units were deployed to France. Here personnel pose with a Scout C at Waddington, one of the training units to take USAS personnel. (Peter Green Collection)

Right: Among the types chosen to be licence-built in the United States was the DH4, although it was to be powered by a Liberty engine. Despite early problems with the match, the type went on to be used in the bomber role with some success. This Liberty-engined DH4 is 'somewhere in France' during 1918. (Andy Thomas Collection)

Below: DH4 of the 89th Squadron at Chatillon-sur-Seine in August 1918. (Andy Thomas Collection)

Above: **The 135th Squadron was one of the pursuit (fighter) squadrons to use the Spad XIII.** (Andy Thomas Collection)

Above: **Sopwith 1½ Strutter with the USAS.** (Peter Green Collection)

Below: **Captain David Peterson with his Nieuport 28 of the 103rd Squadron.** (Ken Delve Collection)

Above: **The 96th Squadron was one of a number of Allied bomber units to operate the Breguet 14-B2.** (Ken Delve Collection)

Right: **Breguet 14 of the 96th Squadron being loaded with bombs at Amanty, 29 July 1918. Maj. J.L. Dunsworth is on the right.** (IWM Q69603)

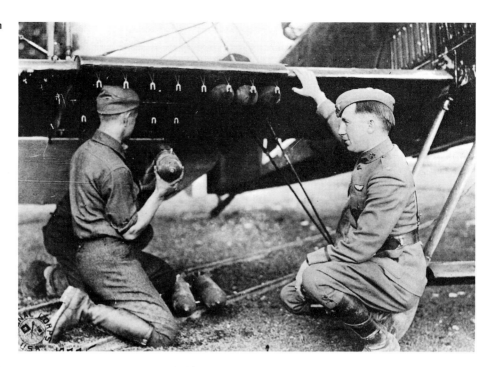

Above: **Salmson SA-2 of the 1st Aero Squadron and DH4s of the 85th Squadron at Toul in late 1918.** (Dennis Hylands)

Left: **Several USAS squadrons used the Salmson 2A2.** (Jack Bruce/Stuart Leslie collection)

Opposite page: **Fokker DVIIs of JG2 at Chery-les-Pouilly, late 1918.** (Alex Imrie)

Left: **Crews of Jasta 62, June 1918: Uffz. Burnitz, Lt. Hagen, Staffelführer Lt. Tönjes, Lt. Näther, Offstv. Sporbert, Uffz. Engler.** (*Freitag*)

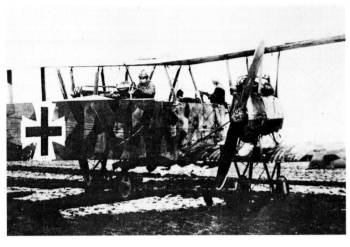

Left: **Gotha GV bombers flew night attacks on Britain from mid 1917 to May 1918, the normal bomb load being 660lb (300kg). The type was not produced in large numbers and it was only moderately effective.** (Ken Wixey Collection)

Right: **Coudekerque airfield, 16 August 1918 – the craters are from a Gotha raid on the night of 5/6 June.** (Ken Delve Collection)

Above left: The Staaken RXIV was an improved version of the RVI, with four 350hp Austro-Daimler engines. R43/17, the first of the type, flew in February 1918 and the few operational aircraft saw active service in late summer 1918. One aircraft, R43, was operating with RFa 501 on the night of 10/11 August when it was shot down. (Ken Delve Collection)

Above right: The German strategic bombing campaign against London continued into 1918. Zeppelin-Staaken RXV R47 was one of three of this variant to see operational service, the first, R46, having been delivered in August 1917. (MAP)

Centre left: 50 Squadron received its first Camels in May 1918 as part of an effort to boost the Home Defence squadrons' capabilities to combat day and night raiders. (Ken Delve Collection)

Below left: As a Home Defence squadron from its formation in May 1916, 50 Squadron took part in the war against airships and bombers – as expressed in this squadron cartoon. (Ken Delve Collection)

Above: Despite early fears in some quarters that the type could not be used for night fighting, 44 Squadron had been the first Home Defence unit to equip with the Camel and proved that it was quite safe and effective. This shot of B2402 is at Hainault Farm, which the squadron occupied from July 1917 to July 1919. (Peter Green Collection)

Right: **An SE5a of 39 Squadron.** (Ken Delve Collection)

Below: **Marham was in use as a Home Defence station, for part of 51 Squadron, from 1916 – note the airfield name adjacent to the circle. Nearby was the RFC station at Narborough, a large and important training base.** (Ken Delve Collection)

167

Above: **Trench lines and a burnt-out village in this reconnaissance photograph taken on 28 September 1918.** (Ken Delve Collection)

Left: **Oblique of 17 September 1918.** (Ken Delve Collection)

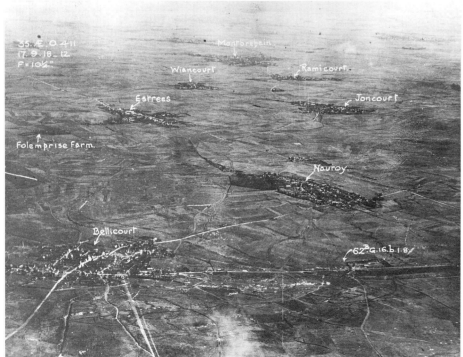

Right: **DH9 D3007 with partial bomb load.** (Peter Green Collection)

Left: **Pensive and well wrapped up, the crew of this 98 Squadron DH9 await the next mission; the observer is Lt. F.J. Keble.** (Ken Delve Collection)

Below: **The Allied bombing offensive increased in scale and effectiveness from the summer of 1918; the formation of the Independent Air Force (more usually known simply as the Independent Force) created an impressive strategic bombing arm with its own fighter units. The DH9, despite its limitations, was one of the most numerous of bomber types in service at the end of the war –some 1,866 being on strength in October.** (Harry Holmes)

169

Right: **Losses among the day bomber units were high; although German fighters did not often cross Allied lines they were quite effective at countering the deep penetration bombing raids. This photo shows British prisoners at Karlsruhe, including, on the right, a 98 Squadron crew (2nd Lt. A.P. Bruce and 2nd Lt. H.H. Rolfe) shot down while attacking the Kirson railway target on 23 October in DH9 D3262.** (Ken Delve Collection)

Left: **Although over 800 Airco DH9As had been accepted by the RAF before the Armistice, only four Squadrons were fully operational. The type was developed for bomber-reconnaissance and showed great promise; indeed it had a good post-war career. F1019 was operational with 99 Squadron, one of the squadrons of the Independent Force.** (Peter Green Collection)

Below: **DH9A E8553 was on charge with 155 Squadron, one of the new day bomber units formed for service in France; however, the war ended before the unit became operational.** (Capt D.S. Glover)

170

Above: The decision to develop a true strategic bombing capability led to a series of long-range heavy bombers. The HP 0/400 followed the HP 0/100 into production as the RAF developed its strategic bombing doctrine – capability. (Ken Delve Collection)

Above: **Lt. Loftus of 100 Squadron in the front turret of an HP 0/400 in France, September 1918. The bomber was defended by five Lewis guns.** (Ken Delve Collection)

Right: **HP 0/400 at Lympne awaiting the ferry flight to France.** (Peter Green Collection)

Above: **HP 0/400** (Ken Delve Collection)

Right: **Bombs burst on an airfield during an attack by 98 Squadron on 3 October 1918.** (Ken Delve Collection)

Left: **Raid in progress by DH4s of 57 Squadron on Moislaines airfield on 8 August 1918 – note the exploding bombs, craters and damage to at least one aircraft.** (Ken Delve Collection)

Right: **Another rail target to the south-east of Cambrai is hit by 98 Squadron on 3 September 1918. This attack was in support of the Battle of the Scarpe: 18 bombs – all 112lb (50kg) – were dropped and the Squadron claimed nine direct hits. One aircraft was shot down by anti-aircraft fire but when the formation was attacked by six Fokker DVIIs they claimed to have driven three of the attackers down out of control.** (Ken Delve Collection)

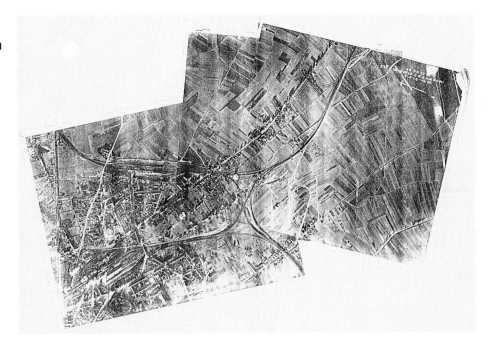

Below: **Rail facilities remained one of the principal targets for the bombers; here bombs burst at Etricourt 14 August 1918.** (Ken Delve Collection)

Above: **The DH10 first flew in March 1918 but development was slow and the type was entering production just as the war ended.** (*FlyPast* Collection)

Left: **A reconnaissance photo of Roules railway junction on 20 May 1918 – it was attacked by four aircraft of 98 Squadron the next day.** (Ken Delve Collection)

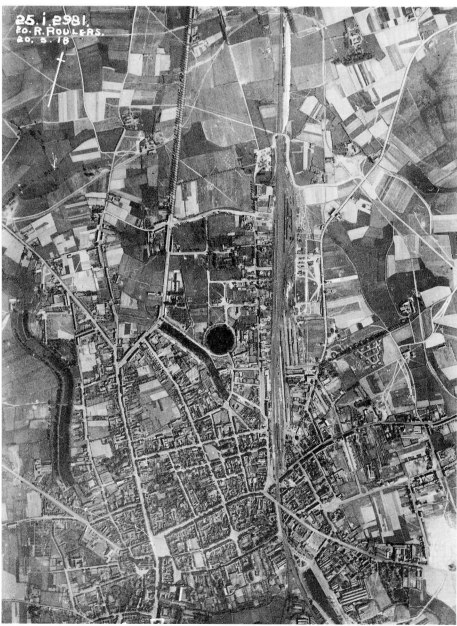

Right: **Operations on the Isonzo Front in Italy continued throughout 1918 and the Italian SIA 7B continued to operate in the reconnaissance role until the summer.** (Peter Green Collection)

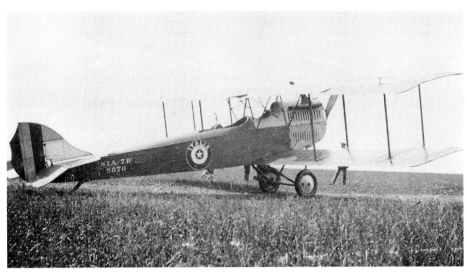

Below: **Caproni bombers were among the first of the true strategic aircraft and, in various forms, were operational throughout the war with a number of Allied air forces.** (*FlyPast* Collection)

Right: **SIA R2 with 270hp Fiat engine**. (IWM Q68810)

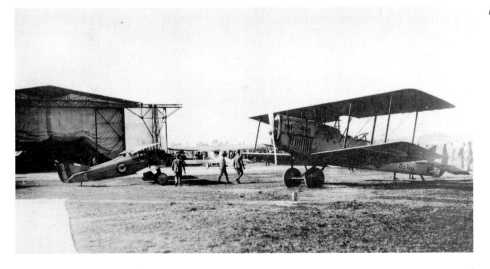

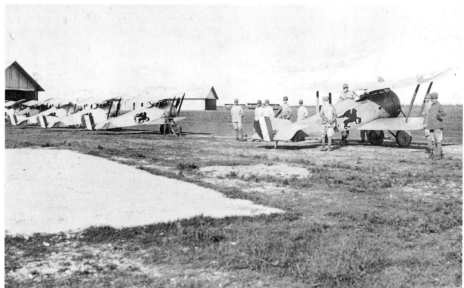

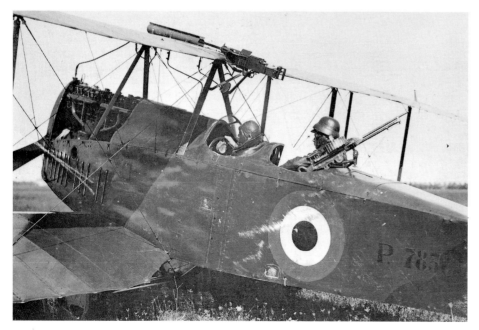

Left: **The SAML was another of the efficient Italian reconnaissance machines that saw active service in 1917 and 1918.** (IWM Q68811)

Right: **Maachi-built Hanriot HD1 fighters; despite producing some excellent bombers and reconnaissance aircraft, the Italians continued to rely on licence-building fighters.** (IWM Q68814)

Below: **Pomilio at Campodi Marcon; this was the second variant with a 270hp Fiat D engine. The Pomilio series was built in large numbers during 1917 and 1918 with some 30 plus squadrons being equipped.** (IWM Q68826)

Above: **Nieuport 27s in Italian service.** (*FlyPast* Collection)

Left: A number of Allied Squadrons deployed to Italy to help bolster the air assets during periods when the Austrians were dominant. This photograph is captioned 'Italy 1918 and a line-up of 45 Squadron camels'. The unit moved to Italy in December 1917 and stayed there until the following September but this may have been taken in France before their departure. (Ken Delve Collection)

Right: Sopwith Baby N1034 was operational with 6 Wing RNAS at Otranto from June 1917 to spring 1918. (Peter Green Collection)

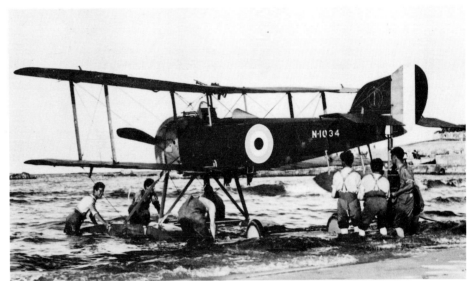

Below: Maj. W.G. Barker poses with Camel B6313 of 139 Squadron. The squadron had formed at Villaveria, Italy in July 1918 and this was the only Camel in an otherwise Bristol Fighter-equipped unit. (Peter Green Collection)

Above left: Godwin Brumowski was the top-scoring Austrian pilot with 35 confirmed victories by the end of the war. (Kostrba)

Above right: Albatros DIII of Austrian ace Godwin Brumowski showing the combat damage the aircraft received on 1 February 1918. (Meindl)

Below: Lloyd CIII of Fliegerkompanie 26 with crew Kpl. Franz Schwarz and Lt. Lambert Hübner. (*FlyPast* Collection)

Right: **Ufag-built Brandenburg CI of Fliegerkompanie 36 with a selection of weapons.** (Grosz)

Below: **226 Squadron Camels at Taranto; the unit was formed from a number of RNAS Flights in April 1918 and was involved in a variety of roles over and around the Adriatic.** (Andy Thomas Collection)

Left: **Aviatik DI of Fliegerkompanie 74J June 1918.** (Grosz)

Above left: **Bristol M1C monoplanes were based with 72 Squadron in Mesopotamia during the early part of 1918. The Squadron flew reconnaissance and fighter mission from a number of LGs over a wide operational area.** (Peter Green Collection)

Above right: **Based at Junction Station, with a detachment at Mudros, 144 Squadron was heavily engaged on operations against the Turks. Here DH9 C6297 has force-landed on return from a raid on 16 September 1918.** (Andy Thomas Collection)

Above: **Anti-submarine patrols were as important in the Mediterranean as they were around the UK and a number of specialist Flights were formed to perform these duties. Four such Flights (Nos. 360 to 363) were based at Calafrana, Malta, and in August 1918 joined to form 267 Squadron. Felixstowe F2a N4488 served with this unit.** (Peter Green Collection)

Left: **Bristol Fighter with Capt. Ross Smith and Lt. E.A. Munster of 1 (Australian) Squadron – this unit had operated Brisfits in the Middle East from February 1918.** (*FlyPast* Collection)

Opposite: **The war is over by Christmas, but four years later than predicted – 49 Squadron celebrate their first Christmas at peace.** (Ken Delve Collection)

49 SQUADRON

MENU

In the Field.

Christmas 1918

Squadron.

Wing.

G.H.Q

Bolo.

Hors D'Oeuvres.
?

Potage.
Consomme P.924.

Entree.
New Turkey 1817 A.D.
Mutton Bones.

Légumes.
Brussel "Flappers"
Pommes "Granite" (small.)
Pomme de terre

Savoury.
"Filles" on Toast.

Entremets
Tarté "Chu Chin Chow"
Ye Olde Christmas Sickness

Café

Hot Air

Cheese.   Butter
Huntley & Palmers "Naughty Wife"
Cigarettes. etc.

Chronology

This is not intended to be a complete chronology of the First World War, but concentrates on the air-related events – most of which are covered in the main body of the text.

July 1914
28   Austria-Hungary declares war on Serbia – the First World War starts.

August 1914
8   Germany Army Zeppelin Z6 bombs Belgian targets, hit by AAA, crashes near Bonn.
13   First two RFC squadrons sent to France.
14   First French attack on Germany; Voisin (Cesari/Prudhommeau) bombs Metz.
19   First operation by RFC, two aircraft on reconnaissance.
22   First RFC aircraft shot down – Avro 504 of 5 Squadron to ground fire over Belgium.
25   2 Squadron, RFC, aircraft forces down first German aircraft.
25   Airship LZ25 bombs Anvers killing civilians.
30   German Taube bombs Paris (Lt. von Hiddessen).

September 1914
3   RNAS made responsible for Home Defence of UK.
8   Capt. P. Nesterov rams Austrian aircraft.
15   First RFC photographic reconnaissance sortie.
15   First operational use of wireless telegraphy.
17   Japanese seaplanes of 2nd Japanese Naval Squadron bomb German ships at Kiaochow.
22   First British bombing of Germany; RNAS attack airship sheds at Düsseldorf.
28   German Air Service adopts 'Iron Cross' insignia.

October 1914
5   First aircraft shot down; Aviatik by Voisin (Frantz/Quénault).
8   Flt. Lt. Marix destroys LZ-25 at Düsseldorf.
19   Maj. W. Siegert appointed as air adviser to German High Command.
26   RNAS aircraft ordered to display insignia based on Union Flag.

November 1914
21   Friedrichshafen raid by RNAS.
23   French form first specialist bomber unit – GB1.

December 1914
10   Russians form EVK with four-engine Ilya Muromets bombers.
12   Imperial German Navy forms first seaplane unit.
11   RNAS adopts roundel as insignia.
24   First aircraft attack on UK, bombs fall near Dover.

January 1915
19   First Zeppelin raid on England.

February 1915
15   First operational use of Ilya Muromets bomber by EVK.
18   German sea blockade of the UK in force.

March 1915
10   British use bombing of railways to support ground operations.
11   First night bombing mission by RFC; two BE2bs bomb Lille.

April 1915
1   Roland Garros scores first victory with machine gun firing through propeller.

May 1915
25   Austrian bombers attack Venice.
31   First airship attack on London, by LZ-38.

June 1915
7   Sub. Lt. Reginald Warneford shoots down LZ-37, awarded VC.

July 1915
25   Victoria Cross awarded to Capt. Lanoe Hawker; first for air combat.

August 1915
12   First successful torpedo attack; Short 184 in Dardanelles.
19   Col. H.M. Trenchard as GOC 'RFC in the Field.'
25   First Italian bombing raid, by Ca32.

February 1916
7   RFC forms first single-seat fighter unit, with DH2s.
10   Responsibility for Home Defence of Britain transferred to RFC from Admiralty.

March 1916
21 Escadrille Américaine formed (later becoming Escadrille Lafayette).

April 1916
15 Start of sustained supply dropping to garrison at Kut El Amara (ends 29 April).

July 1916
15 RFC forms Middle East Brigade, HQ Egypt.

August 1916
10 Jagdstaffel 2 formed, first such fighter unit.
29 US Naval Flying Corps formed.

September 1916
2/3 First Zeppelin shot down over UK by 2nd Lt. W. Leefe Robinson – awarded VC.
15 First submarine sunk by air attack, French Foucault to Austrian Lohner.

October 1916
25 Luftstreitkräfte (German Air Force) formed.
28 Death of Oswald Boelcke.

November 1916
3 First HP 0/100 to 3 Wing RNAS.
23 Death of Lanoe Hawker.
25 German Air Service becomes separate military branch.

January 1917
7 VC to Sgt. T.T. Mottershead.

May 1917
20 U-36 sunk by Large America; first German submarine sunk by aircraft.
25 First mass Gotha raid on UK, by Kaghol 3.

June 1917
2 VC to 'Billy' Bishop.
13 First mass Gotha raid on London.

August 1917
2 First landing of an aircraft on a ship under way, by Sqn. Cdr. E.H. Dunning on HMS *Furious*.

September 1917
2/3 First mass night raid on UK by Gothas.
11 Death of Georges Guynemer.
17 First raid on UK by German Giant bombers.
23 Death of Werner Voss.

January 1918
2 British Air Ministry formed.
26 Trial release of Albatros fighter from airship.

February 1918
18 First American fighter squadron arrives in France: 95th Aero Squadron.

April 1918
1 Formation of Royal Air Force.
11 First US air operation; by 1 Corps observation squadron.
21 Death of Manfred von Richthofen.

May 1918
13 Formation of Independent Air Force.

June 1918
12 First operation by American day bombers; 96th Squadron to Dommany–Baroncourt.

July 1918
6 First operation by Independent Air Force.
9 Death of James McCudden.
10 VC to Capt. F.M.F. West.

October 1918
27 VC to Maj. William Barker.

November 1918
11 End of war.

Aircraft Data

British Aircraft

Aircraft	Role	Crew	IOC	Wing Span	Length	Maximum Speed	Ceiling
BE2c	R	2	1914	40ft 6in	27ft 3in	90mph	9,000ft
RE5	R/B	2	1914	45ft 3½in	26ft 2in	78mph	–
BE8	R	2	1914	39ft 6in	27ft 3in	70mph	–
Sopwith Tabloid	R/B	1	1914	25ft 6in	20ft 4in	92mph	15,000ft
Martinsyde S.1	R/F	1	1914	27ft 8in	21ft	84mph	–
Avro 504A	R/B	2	1914	36ft	29ft 5in	82mph	12,000ft
FB5	F	2	1915	36ft 6in	27ft 2in	70mph	9,000ft
Scout D	F	1	1915	24ft 7in	20ft 8in	100mph	16,000ft
RE7	B	2	1915	57ft 2in	31ft 10½in	85mph	6,500ft
FE2b	R/F	2	1915	47ft 9in	32ft 3in	88mph	9,000ft
DH2	F	1	1916	28ft 3in	25ft 2½in	93mph	14,000ft
FE8	F	1	1916	31ft 6in	23ft	94mph	14,500ft
Sopwith Pup	F	1	1916	26ft 6in	19ft 3¾in	112mph	17,500ft
BE12	F/B	1	1916	37ft	27ft 3in	102mph	12,500ft
Sopwith 1½ Strutter	F/B	1	1916	33ft 6in	25ft 3in	106mph	13,000ft
HP 0/100	B	4	1916	100ft	62ft 10¼in	85mph	7,000ft
RE8	R/B	2	1916	42ft 7in	27ft 10½in	103mph	13,500ft
DH5	F	1	1917	25ft 8in	22ft	102mph	16,000ft
Bristol M1C	F	1	1917	30ft 9in	20ft 4in	130mph	20,000ft
Bristol F2b	F	2	1917	39ft 3in	25ft 10in	125mph	20,000ft
SE5	F	1	1917	27ft 9in	20ft 11in	122mph	19,000ft
SE5a	F	1	1917	26ft 7½in	20ft 11in	138mph	23,000ft
Sopwith Camel	F	1	1917	28ft	18ft 9in	115mph	19,000ft
Sopwith Triplane	F	1	1917	26ft 6in	18ft 10in	117mph	20,500ft
DH4	B	2	1917	42ft 4½in	30ft 8in	143mph	23,500ft
Sopwith Baby	R/B	1	1917	25ft 8in	23ft	100mph	7,600ft
Sopwith Snipe	F	1	1918	30ft	19ft 10in	121mph	19,500ft
Avro 504K	NF	1	1918	36ft	29ft 5in	95mph	16,000ft

French Aircraft

Aircraft	Role	Crew	IOC	Wing Span	Length	Maximum Speed	Ceiling
Blériot XI	R	2	1914	33ft 11in	27ft 10in	66mph	3,280ft
Maurice-Farman II	R/B	2	1914	53ft	30ft 8in	66mph	12,467ft
Henri-Farman 20	R	2	1914	44ft 10in	27ft 9in	65mph	9,022ft

Aircraft	Role	Crew	IOC	Wing Span	Length	Maximum Speed	Ceiling
Morane-Saulnier N	F	1	1914	26ft 8½in	19ft 1½in	90mph	13,123ft
Nieuport 11	F	1	1915	24ft 9in	19ft ⅓in	97mph	15,090ft
Voisin V	B	2	1915	48ft 4¾in	31ft 3¼in	65mph	11,485ft
Caudron G.4	R/B	2	1915	56ft 5in	23ft 6in	82mph	14,110ft
Breguet M5	B	2	1915	57ft 9in	32ft 6in	88mph	14,110ft
FBA Type C	R	2	1915	44ft 11in	28ft 10in	68mph	11,480ft
Nieuport 17	F	1	1916	26ft 10in	18ft 11in	110mph	17,390ft
Spad S.VII	F	1	1916	25ft 6in	20ft 1in	119mph	18,000ft
Voisin 8	B	2	1916	61ft 8in	36ft 2in	82mph	14,110ft
Breguet 14	B	2	1917	47ft 1¼in	29ft	110mph	19,030ft
Hanriot HD.1	F	1	1917	28ft 6½in	19ft 2¼in	115mph	20,670ft
Spad XIII	F	1	1917	26ft 11in	20ft 8in	138mph	21,820ft
Morane-Saulnier A1	F	1	1917	27ft 11in	18ft 6½in	138mph	22,965ft

German and Austrian Aircraft

Aircraft	Role	Crew	IOC	Wing Span	Length	Maximum Speed	Ceiling
DFW B.I	R	2	1914	45ft 11¼in	27ft 6¾in	75mph	9,840ft
Albatros B.II	R	2	1914	42ft	25ft ½in	66mph	9,840ft
AEG B.II	R	2	1914	42ft 7in	25ft 7in	–	–
Lohner E	R	2	1914	53ft 2in	33ft 8in	65mph	13,120ft
Albatros C.I	R	2	1915	42ft 4in	25ft 9in	82mph	9,840ft
LVG C.II	R	2	1915	42ft 4in	26ft 7in	81mph	13,120ft
FF 33	R/F	2	1915	54ft 11½in	34ft 3½in	75mph	10,500ft
Aviatik B.II	R	2	1915	46ft	26ft	68mph	8,140ft
Fokker E.III	F	1	1915	30ft 10½in	23ft 11¼in	87mph	11,500ft
Aviatik C.I	R	2	1915	41ft 0¼in	26ft	89mph	11,480ft
Rumpler C.I	R	2	1915	39ft 10½in	25ft 9in	95mph	16,600ft
AEG G.IV	B	3	1916	60ft 4½in	31ft 10in	103mph	14,760ft
AEG C.IV	R	2	1916	44ft 2in	23ft 5½in	99mph	16,405ft
Albatros C.V	R	2	1916	41ft 11¼in	29ft 4½in	106mph	16,405ft
Hansa-Brandenburg KDW	F	1	1916	30ft 4¼in	26ft 3in	106mph	13,123ft
DFW C.V	R	2	1916	43ft 6⅝in	25ft 10⅛in	97mph	16,400ft
Fokker D.II	F	1	1916	29ft 8lin	20ft 8in	100mph	15,000ft
Hannover CL.II	F/GA	2	1916	38ft 4¾in	24ft 10½in	103mph	24,600ft
LFG Roland C.II	R/F	2	1916	33ft 9½in	25ft 3¼in	103mph	15,000ft
Hansa-Brandenburg W.12	F	2	1916	36ft 9in	31ft 6in	100mph	16,405ft
Albatros D.II	F	1	1916	27ft 10¾in	24ft 3in	109mph	17,060ft
Halberstadt D.II	F	1	1916	28ft 10½in	23ft 11½in	90mph	19,608ft
Aviatik D.I	F	1	1917	26ft 3in	22ft 9½in	115mph	20,177ft
Fokker Dr.I	F	1	1917	23ft 7½in	19ft 11in	103mph	19,685ft
Albatros D.III	F	1	1917	29ft 8¼in	24ft ½in	109mph	18,044ft
Albatros D.Va	F	1	1917	29ft 8¼in	24ft ½in	116mph	18,700ft
Halberstadt CL.II	GA	2	1917	35ft 4in	23ft 11½in	103mph	16,700ft
LFG Roland D.II	F	1	1917	29ft 3in	22ft 8in	105mph	16,500ft
Gotha G.V	B	3	1917	77ft 9¼in	38ft 11in	87mph	21,325ft
Staaken R.VI	B	7	1917	138ft 5½in	72ft 6¼in	84mph	14,170ft

Aircraft	Role	Crew	IOC	Wing Span	Length	Maximum Speed	Ceiling
LVG C.V	R	2	1917	44ft 8½in	26ft 5¾in	103mph	21,300ft
Rumpler C.VII	R	2	1917	41ft 27in	26ft 10⅞in	109mph	24,000ft
Halberstadt C.V	R	2	1918	44ft 8¾in	22ft 8½in	106mph	17,500ft
Phönix C.I	R	2	1918	36ft 1in	24ft 8in	110mph	17,715ft
Hansa-Brandenburg W.2G	F	2	1918	44ft 4in	30ft 8½in	109mph	16,400ft
Fokker D.VII	F	1	1918	29ft 3½in	22ft 11⅝in	117mph	22,900ft

Italian Aircraft

Aircraft	Role	Crew	IOC	Wing Span	Length	Maximum Speed	Ceiling
Caproni Ca.32	B	4	1915	72ft 10in	35ft 9in	32mph	–
SAML S2	R	2	1917	39ft 8½in	27ft 10¾in	101mph	–
SIA 7B.1	R	2	1917	43ft 8½in	29ft 8½in	116mph	22,965ft
Ansaldo SVA.5	R	1	1918	29ft 10¼in	26ft 7in	143mph	21,980ft
Pomilio PE	R	2	1918	38ft 8½in	29ft 4in	120mph	16,405ft
Caproni Ca.46	B	4	1918	76ft 9¼in	41ft 4in	94mph	14,760ft

Key

F = Fighter
B = Bomber
R = Reconnaissance
GA = Ground Attack
NF = Night Fighter

Air Aces

The following tables give basic details of the ten top-scoring pilots from each of the major air arms. There is often dispute as to the exact number of victories an individual obtained; most of the air forces insisted on confirmation of a victory either from the physical presence of the enemy aircraft or at least one eye witness confirmation. Victory scores include balloons.

Britain

Score	Name	Fate
73	Edward Mannock	Killed in action, 26 July 1918
72	William A. Bishop	Survived
60	Raymond Collishaw	Survived
57	James T.B. McCudden	Died in flying accident, 9 July 1918
54	Andrew W. Beauchamp-Proctor	Survived
54	D.R. MacLaren	Survived
53	William G. Barker	Survived
47	Robert A. Little	Killed in action, 27 May 1918
46	P.F. Fullard	Survived
46	G.E. McElroy	Killed in action, 31 July 1918

United States

Score	Name	Fate
26	Eddie V. Rickenbacker	Survived
21	Frank Luke	Killed in action, 27 September 1918
17	Raoul Lufbery	Killed in action, 19 May 1918
13	George A. Vaughn	Survived
12	Field E. Kindley	Survived
12	David E. Putnam	Killed in action, 12 September 1918
12	Elliot W. Springs	Survived
10	Reed G. Landis	Survived
10	Jacques M. Swaab	Survived

Italy

Score	Name	Fate
34	Francesco Baracca	Killed in action, 19 June 1918
26	Silvio Scaroni	Survived
24	Pier R. Piccio	Survived
21	Flavio T. Baracchini	Killed in action, 1918
20	Fulco R. di Calabria	Survived
17	Marziale Cerutti	?
17	Ferreuccio Ranza	Survived
12	Luigi Olivari	Died in flying accident, 13 October 1917
11	Giovanni Ancillotto	?
11	Antonio Reali	?

France

Score	Name	Fate
75	René Fonck	Survived
53	Georges Guynemer	Killed in action, 11 September 1917
43	Charles Nungesser	Survived
41	Georges Madon	Survived
35	Jean Boyau	Killed in action, 14 September 1918
34	Michel Coiffard	Killed in action, 27 October 1918
28	Jean Bourjade	Survived
27	Armand Pinsard	Survived
23	René Dorme	Killed in action, 25 May 1917
23	Gabriel Guérin	Died in flying accident, 1 August 1918

Germany

Score	Name	Fate
80	Manfred von Richthofen	Killed in action, 21 April 1918
62	Ernst Udet	Survived
53	Erich Lowewenhardt	Died in flying accident, 10 August 1918
48	Werner Voss	Killed in action, 23 September 1917
45	Fritz Rumey	Killed in action, 28 September 1918
44	Rudolph Berthold	Survived
43	Paul Bäumer	Survived
41	Josef Jacobs	Survived
41	Bruno Loerzer	Survived
40	Oswald Boelcke	Killed in action, 28 October 1916
40	Franz Büchner	Survived
40	Lothar von Richthofen	Survived

Austria–Hungary

Score	Name	Fate
35	Godwin Brumowski	Survived
32	Julius Arigi	Survived
27	Frank Linke-Crawford	Killed in action, 31 July 1918
28	Beno Fiala	Survived
19	Josef Kiss	Killed in action, 25 May 1918
18	Franz Gräser	Killed in action, 17 May 1918
16	Stefan Fejes	Survived
16	Eugen Bönsch	Survived
15	Ernst Strohschneider	Killed in action, 21 March 1918
12	Adolf Heyrowsky	Survived

Selective Reading List

The 1990s have seen an upsurge in the number of books published on First World War air operations; the series from Grub Street in particular doing much to provide a solid corpus of factual material.

A Short History of the RAF. Air Ministry AP125, 2nd edition, 1936.

United States Air Service in World War One. USAF Office of Air Force History, 1978 (4 volumes).

Abate R., Alegi G. and Apostolo G. *Aeroplani Caproni.* Museo Caproni, 1992.

Bickers R.T. *The First Great Air War.* Hodder and Stoughton, 1988.

Bickers R.T. *Von Richthofen, the Legend Evaluated.* Airlife, 1996.

Bowyer C. *For Valour, the Air VCs.* William Kimber, 1985.

Brooks P. *Zeppelin, the Rigid Airships 1893–1940.* Putnam, 1993.

Bruce J. *The Aeroplanes of the Royal Flying Corps (Military Wing).* Putnam, 1982.

Cole C. *McCudden VC.* William Kimber, 1967.

Cole C. *RAF Communiqués 1915–16.* Tom Donovan Publishing, 1990.

Cole C. *RAF Communiqués 1918.* Tom Donovan Publishing, 1990.

Cross R. *The Bombers.* Bantam Press, 1987.

Cuich M. *De l'Aeronautique Militaire 1912 à l'Armee de l'Air 1976.*

Delve K. *Night Fighter.* Arms and Armour, 1995.

Delve K. *The Winged Bomb (39 Squadron).* Midland Counties, 1985.

Franks N. *Who Downed the Aces in World War One?* Grub Street, 1996.

Franks N., Bailey F. *Over the Front.* Grub Street, 1992.

Franks N., Baley F. and Duiven R. *The Jasta Pilots.* Grub Street, 1996.

Franks N., Guest R. and Bailey F. *Above the Lines.* Grub Street, 1993.

Franks N., Guest R. and Bailey F. *Bloody April. Black September.* Grub Street, 1995.

Gray P. and Thetford O. *German Aircraft of the First World War.* Putnam, 1962.

Grosz P., Haddow G. and Schiemer. *Austro-Hungarian Army Aircraft of World War One.* Flying Machines Press, 1993.

Haddow G. and Grosz P. *The German Giants.* Putnam, 1988.

Halley J.J. *Squadrons of the RAF and Commonwealth.* Air Britain, 1988.

Hare P. *The Royal Aircraft Factory.* Putnam, 1990.

Haute A. van. *French Air Force 1909–40.*

Henshaw T. *The Sky their Battlefield.* Grub Street, 1995.

Hiscock M. *Classic Aircraft of World War One.* Osprey, 1994.

Imrie A. *German Fighter Units 1914–1917.* Osprey, 1978.

Kilduff P. *Germany's First Air Force.* William Kimber, 1979.

Kilduff P. *Over the Battlefronts.* Arms and Armour 1996.

Kilmarx R. *A History of Soviet Air Power.* Faber and Faber, 1962.

Layman R. *Naval Aviation in the First World War.* Chatham Publishing, 1996.

Lewis C. *Sagittarius Rising.* Greenhill, 1993.

Lewis G.H. *Wings over the Somme 1916–18.* Bridge Books, 1994.

Morrow J.H. *The Great War in the Air.* Airlife, 1993.

Mowthorpe C. *Battlebags, British Airships of the First World War.* Alan Sutton, 1995.

Neumann P. *The German Air Force in the Great War.* Hodder and Stoughton, 1920.

O'Connor M. *Air Aces of the Austro-Hungarian Empire 1914–1918.* Champlin Fighter Press, 1986.

Revell A. *Arthur Rhys Davids.* William Kimber.

Richthofen M. von. *The Red Air Fighter.* Greenhill, 1990.

Rickenbacker E. *Fighting the Flying Circus.* Doubleday, 1965.

Rimmel R.B. *Zeppelin!* Conway Maritime Press, 1984.

Rimmel R.B. *Airship VC.* Aston Publications, 1988.

Rimmel R.B. *World War One Survivors.* Aston Publications, 1990.

Robertson B. *Air Aces of the 1914–18 War.* Harleyford, 1959.

Robertson B. *British Military Aircraft Serials 1878–1987.* Midland Counties, 1987.

Snowden Gamble C.F. *The Story of a North Sea Air Station.* Neville Spearman, 1967.

Sturtivant R. and Page G. *Royal Naval Aircraft Serials and Units 1911–19.* Air Britain, 1992.

Sturtivant R. and Page G. *The Camel File.* Air Britain, 1993.

Thayer L.H. *America's First Eagles.* Bender Publishing, 1983.

Thetford O. *Aircraft of the Royal Air Force.* Putnam, 1988.

Thetford O. *British Naval Aircraft Since 1912.* Putnam, 1991.

White C. *The Gotha Summer.* Hale, 1986.

Whitehouse A. *The Zeppelin Fighters.* Robert Hale, 1966.

Journals

Over the Front – Journal of World War One Aviation Historians

Cross and Cockade International

Air Enthusiast

Windsock

Windsock Datafiles

Index

Index